Understanding the Power of Prayer

UNDERSTANDING
the
POWER
of
PRAYER

EXPERIENCING THE POWER TO
CHANGE YOUR WORLD.

BY

JEMIRIYE P. FAKUNLE

XULON PRESS

Xulon Press
2301 Lucien Way #415, Maitland, FL 32751, 407.339.4217
www.xulonpress.com

Paperback ISBN-13: 978-1-66286-069-0
Ebook ISBN-13: 978-1-66286-070-6

TO

---

*Grace, helpmeet and friend
with whom I have learned, proved and
tested these principles in
real situations.*

ACKNOWLEDGMENTS

I AM GRATEFUL to the people of Blue Mound United Methodist Church. This book was inspired by a series of sermons shared with this congregation. They are a peculiarly remarkable congregation and I am blessed to serve as their pastor.

Also, I have a wonderful community of people that needs to take credit for this book. Sometimes people deserve credit because they walk with us in bringing out the best in us. Sometimes, they are praiseworthy because they have provided the right encouragement and motivation we need to keep going when we think we have no strength left. In other cases, we need to share credit with people because they have sacrificed a part of their lives to see our dreams come through.

I would like to thank Peggy Ramert, a faithful follower of Christ, whose love for me and my family is praiseworthy. A shout-out to my friend, Segun Arobadi, who has been an inspiration and whose faith has been a source of courage and strength for me in life and ministry.

Special thanks to Iyabo Onipede, Evan Hill, Anita Munden, and Sarah Isbell, their help in editorial revisions and encouraging feedback has made this book possible. Your labor of love shall never be forgotten.

I am indebted to my parents Deborah and Moses Fakunle, for guiding my path early in life in following Christ. Their faith now lives in me and has become a source of inspiration to many across the globe.

To our children TiOluwanimi, Oluwateniola, Oluwatomini, and OreofeOluwasimi, you all are a joy and delight. I am thankful to have children who love to hear Daddy preach and to whom I owe the responsibility of bequeathing a legacy of the faith that was once delivered unto us.

Finally, my partner, wife, and best friend, Grace Fakunle, has shaped my life and faith. With her I have experienced some of the truth shared in this book, and she has been a strong pilar of strength in my life and ministry, and for our children as well. Thank you for all your sacrifice and support, it's a privilege to have you as a Treasure!

CONTENTS

CONTENTS

INTRODUCTION

"God shapes the world by prayer"– E.M. Bounds[1]

E.M. Bounds' quote above offers a compelling purpose for developing an effective and productive prayer life. Without a doubt, God has created perfect earth on which we move and live. And by His own judgment, all that God made was good. However, we cannot say the same thing for the world because there's the world out there, there's your own world, and there's my own world, and our worlds are not the same. We live in different worlds across race, political leanings, educational advancement, socio-economic status, and religious beliefs. While the earth is rich and nature is beautiful and fierce, we live in a world of the rich and poor, princes and peasants, the mighty and the weak, the wise and the foolish. With its different levels of experiences, we are called to live as Christians and citizens of heaven in this world. We are called to demonstrate divine abilities above the inequalities, prejudices, and endless vices of human wickedness and the evils constantly crafted by the kingdom of darkness.

I believe that prayer is one sure path we need to walk as Christians to demonstrate divine abilities today. Through prayer, we can align ourselves with God and manifest the brightness of His glory over the powers of darkness and human wickedness. Psalm 115:6 says, **"The heaven, even the heavens, are the Lord's; But the earth He has given to the children of men" (NKJV).** If the above Scripture is true, it means the Sovereign God has chosen to partner with us so we can be the extension of His dominion on the face of the earth. And the great privilege of Christians, as I see it, is to partner with God through a lifestyle of prayer. God desires to cooperate with humanity in governing creation, so God saved humanity through Jesus Christ, who is God and human. As Christians, Christ taught us to pray that the kingdom of God will come to the earth and that God's will be done on the earth as it is in heaven. Prayer then is the vehicle for our cooperation with God and the means that grant us the capacity to shape our world. Prayer allows us to know God's will, not just in general, but in the particulars of our lives, even down to daily decisions. So, I agree with E.M. Bounds that "God shapes the world by prayer."

Christ, our Lord, informs us before His passion about what to expect in the world and from the world. In John 16:33, He says, **"I have told you these things, so that in Me you may have (perfect) peace. In the world you have**

tribulations and distress and suffering, but be coura-geous (be confident, be undaunted, be filled with joy); I have overcome the world. (My conquest is accom-plished, My victory abiding)" (Amp). The text above gives us the reason to shape our own world and the world around us through the victory secured by Christ. The way to access that victory is through the power of prayer. Suppose we are not going to be daunted and be victim-ized by the tribulations and distresses of the world. In that case, we need to know how to live through the conquest that Christ has accomplished for us. Therefore, I wrote this book to encourage and challenge you to choose not to live a victimized life. I write to challenge your heart to be willing to grasp all the advantages that prayer offers.

As someone from a humble background and who grew up in one of the most densely populated counties in Lagos, Nigeria, I learned early about my need to shape my world. In a society where the government preys on the citizens and the rich rule perpetually over the poor. I learned that my choices were to either give in to the debilitating effect of poverty or shape my own world through the power of prayer. I knew that if I joined the company of those who complain about how bad life is treating them and how they have no one to help, I would have many regrets in old age. To avoid this, I choose the way of prayer so I can know how to live my life to the fullest, serve God and ful-fill my God-given destiny.

Meanwhile, having lived in the United States for the last seven years, I know that Western society's comfort and ease are temporal and sometimes superficial. I have seen that people still suffer pain amid comfort, and many are still poor amid abundance. I know that many live under the bondage of sicknesses and diseases despite all the advancements science and technology offer. So, either here or there, the world we live in is bedeviled by powers beyond our human capacities. Therefore, we must learn how to run to the name of the Lord, where we can find true salvation.

So, this book is a call to action. It's for anyone and everyone who desires to know the Lord deeply and intimately. My burden is to sound out God's call to prayer in your ears until you can respond to the rhythm of the sound and take your place in the assembly of the saints that calls upon God in Spirit and in truth. It doesn't matter where you are in the world. You can create your own world and live above the intimidations from the powers of darkness, corruption, and vices that penetrate the fabrics of society. If your desire is to live for Christ and live the conqueror's life as you serve God and His people, this book is for you. You will find the pages in this book reviving, refreshing, renewing, and revealing. Anyone passionate about seeing how the church can beat back the forces of hell militating against God's kingdom and purposes will find this book instructional and empowering. If you have been discouraged by unanswered prayer, I encourage you to read with your heart open, and you will yet see the salvation of God. The God we serve is the God who answers prayers, and in the pages of this book, you'll learn that while God shapes the world by prayer, our prayer must be shaped by the word of God. When this happens, we will see the manifest power of God again, and we will become empowered to walk in the miraculous and the supernatural. Through the power of prayer, we can build strength and find the will to serve God's purpose until the kingdom of this world becomes **"The kingdom of our Lord and His Christ, and He shall reign forever and ever" (Revelation 11:15b, NKJV).**

Understanding the Power of Prayer has eight chapters carefully arranged to help you ascend in your spirit into the place where God promises to bless the seeking soul. Chapter One answers the question, "Why Do We Pray?" In it, you will discover that we lose more than we gain when we fail to pray. In Chapter Two, I write about "Prayer as a Spiritual Exercise." As you read, you will learn that we need God's help to truly call upon His name. You will see how you can take advantage of God's provision available to help us lead a practical prayer life. Chapter Three speaks about "Of Prayer Length," where I explained that prayer has no ideal or predetermined length. Our job is not just to pray but to build a lifestyle of prayer, and we are to pray until we see results.

In Chapter Four, about prayers that produce results, I write, "You Can Have What You Ask For." In it, you will learn of the faithfulness of our God and how if we seek Him on His own terms, we will have what we ask for in prayer. In Chapter Five, I write about "Prayer and Faith." In it, you will see what biblical faith means and how you can apply it in your life and experience our prayer-answering God in His power and glory. Chapter Six is where I write about "Prayer Patterns," In it, you will learn from men like Daniel and Elijah, who subdued the powers of darkness through their faith and prayer. The lives of these men will challenge you to rise in mighty victory and fight the good fight of faith from the position of victory. Finally, in the last two chapters, I bring the prayer practice of Christ to the front and speak about the sole and authentic goal of building an effective prayer life. I explicate that through prayer, we can discover, embrace, and function in life in ways that are congruent to who we are in Christ. In these two chapters, you will learn from Jesus' practice of prayer and grasp what He prayed about. You will discover that we have no better model of prayer than this. If you can align and shape your prayer in the order of Christ, you will access the same power that made Christ a threat to the kingdom of darkness. Each chapter of the book comes with prayer points. I encourage you to take advantage of these points to revive, renew, establish, and reestablish a formidable and indomitable prayer life. With prayer, you can shape your world according to the plans of God for your life. These prayer points are carefully arranged in the appendix.

Whether you are a new believer or an old saint, it is with great humility that I commit this book to your hands. As you read, may revival break forth within your spirit. May the power of the Holy Spirit fill you afresh. May you be baptized with the Spirit of grace and supplication. May your life serve all the purposes of God. And may you experience God's mighty salvation in all areas of your life and endeavors in Jesus' name, AMEN!

Your Brother,
Jemiriye Fakunle

CHAPTER ONE:

WHY PRAY?

"¹I will love You, O LORD, my strength. ²The LORD is my rock and my fortress and my deliverer; My God, my strength, in whom I will trust; My shield and the horn of my salvation, my stronghold. ³I will call upon the Lord, who is worthy to be praised; So shall I be saved from my enemies."
(Psalm 18:1-3, NKJV)

In the world today, there are many different attitudes toward prayer. While some people believe in the power encapsulated in prayer, others don't believe in God, let alone in the power of praying to God. Many of us in the church have experienced what prayer can do at different levels and in different dimensions. Yet, some of us have been frustrated about not receiving answers. For others, prayer is something we do to make us feel good about our religiosity.

Christopher Hitchens, the author of **God Is Not Great: Why Religion Poisons Everything,** was 62 when he was undergoing chemotherapy for his throat cancer. Now deceased, he was famous for his atheism. The title of his book reveals the author's attitude toward God. Yet, many Christians prayed for his healing during his chemotherapy. To those who prayed for his recovery, Hitchens offers the following opinion, "I think of it as a nice gesture. And it may well make them feel better, which is a good thing in itself."[2] Is this what we think of prayer? Is prayer nothing more than a nice gesture that makes us feel better about ourselves? Is there any legitimate, life-transforming reason to pray? What can prayer do for you and for your family? What can prayer do for a people and for a nation? I encourage you to hold these questions in your heart as you read on.

Myles Munroe has been credited with saying, "When the purpose is not known, abuse is inevitable."[3] I think this statement applies to the concept of prayer. There are different categories of Christians today with different attitudes and dispositions toward prayer. First, many professing believers today think they know what prayer is without knowing what prayer is. So, when you take a cursory and closer look at their lives, you will hardly find the marks accompanying those who pray. Second, some Christians labor so much in prayer but get a little result because they pray amiss and without power. For these Christians, you will sometimes hear them speak proudly about their prayer life. Still, for the discerning spirit, it's not difficult to see that their talk is empty and void of the presence and power of God available for those who pray. Many prayer houses are full of people like this. Their prayers make so much noise but constitute little to nothing before the Lord. They utter so many words in prayer, but their prayer gains very little mileage in the realm of the spirit. Third, there are some Christians whose understanding of prayer convinces them that God ought not to be bothered about our needs. They believe that if God wants to do something for believers, He will do so without us asking Him. I have met such Christians before. A pastor once told me that their denomination does not believe in healing by demand, and if God wants to heal, He will do so of His own accord. It took me a while to comprehend our conversation. Such a belief system hides under the notion of **"Your kingdom come"** and forgets the rest of that statement that says, **"Your will be done on earth as it is in heaven,"** **(Matthew 6:10, NKJV).** For many believers today, the point is that the will of God in prayer has become reduced to an abstract concept. They have made the will of God look irrelevant and impracticable in real-time, in real situations, and for real people.

If you are one such Christian living under the influence of such a system, I invite you to keep an open heart as you read through the following pages. The Lord has something to say to you, and the only way you will hear it is by keeping an open heart. Read with your heart and resist the reluctance that comes with over-rationalizing the word of God. The matter of prayer is a matter of the heart and not a thing to stuff the head with. To profit richly from spiritual matters, we must allow the mass of our faith to outweigh our rational abilities. Don't rationalize away the truth established in the Scriptures about the potency and power of prayer in a believer's life.

There's the fourth category of believers who miss the purpose and benefit of prayer. These Christians genuinely understand what prayer can do doctrinally but have little experiential knowledge. They pray but quit too soon before the depths of God can open to them. Such individuals begin to see the drops of mercies falling around them, and they settle too quickly in the shallow waters. They fail to understand that God wants them to experience the outpouring showers of His mercies. They ignore God's desires to drench them with the rain of His blessings and leave indelible marks on their spiritual pilgrimage as a people who know how to call upon the name of the Lord. Yet, there's a fifth category of believers, but their numbers are few. These are believers who have learned the culture of prayer as a lifestyle. They have resolved only to function by God; their desire is to live for the will of God and be the true reflection of the life of Christ in spirit and power. To this end, I invite you to come with me and explore how we can live in the will of God through prayer and manifest the more than conquerors' life in the world, in our worlds today.

I don't know where you stand in the categories described above. Still, I hope you can be stirred heavenward to ascend to heights you've never experienced through the power of prayer. I hope a cry rises loudly within your heart for the Lord to teach you how to pray and empower you to pray. But, above all, I pray you will resist every thought attempting to lift itself above the revelational truth God wants you to see in the pages of this book.

Why Do We Pray…?

For a believer in Christ, one sure way of establishing spiritual truth is by diving and digging deep into the pages of the Scriptures under the beaming light of the Holy Spirit. If you do so, you'll find that Scripture is replete with stories of men and women who know a thing or two about the power of prayer. Some prayed and got results, while some of them prayed, but their prayers failed to move the hands of God. To the former, prayer ceases to be a mystery. Instead, prayer is the transport of ascension into the very throne room of God, where God becomes real, and His power is released to show them great and mighty things. David is one such individual who understood the secret but revealed the power of prayer. So, let's briefly explore what David has to say about why we pray from Psalm 18 and from 2 Samuel 22, its parallel chapter, and its context. Psalm 18 is a song of testimony that attests to the efficacious power of prayer in real-life situations. This song of David confirms that there is hope for the man and woman who can call upon the Lord. Here's what the texts say:

"Then David spoke to the Lord the words of this song, on the day when the Lord had delivered him from the hand of all his enemies, and from the hand of Saul." (2 Samuel 22:1, NKJV)

"I will call upon the Lord, who is worthy to be praised; So shall I be saved from my enemies." (Psalm 18:3, NKJV)

These are all statements from a man who has learned the dynamics of prayer. In these utterances lay the path to a victorious Christian life. David brings us into the prayer closet of a man the Bible describes as a **"Man after God's heart"** (1Samuel 13:44, NKJV). Here's what's clear from David's opening statement above; The God of the Bible is a God who delivers. The God the Scripture reveals is the God of Angel Armies. He has the capacity and capability to deliver believers from all their enemies and from the hands of the mighty. So, as we seek to find Scriptural answers to why we should pray, let's be aware and assure that the God unto whom we pray still delivers, saves, heals, blesses, and strengthens. There's no power beside Him and no might beyond Him. Our God is the King over all the ends of the earth (Psalm 47:2), and He shall deliver His people and make them possess their inheritance. From the preceding, we have hope and the sure word of promises that if David could sing God's song of deliverance, we would sing God's song of redemption. Our God has not changed and will never change. He reigns!

To make the conversation about why we pray clearer, let's see the rendering of Psalm 18:3 in the Common English Bible (CEB):

"Because he is praiseworthy, I cried out to the Lord, and I was saved from my enemies" (CEB)

In the CEB version above, we see two factors that should drive our adventures in prayer. More reasons will be explored later in this book, but these two factors will suffice. The first reason is that our God is praiseworthy. Any belief in prayer and any activity done in prayer must begin with the reverent awareness that there is no power, might, dominion, or authority outside of God that deserves our worship and praise. We turn to the Lord in prayer because God alone is the Rock, and everything outside of Him is sinking sand. Elsewhere, the Psalmist declares, **"You are more glorious and excellent than the mountains of prey" (Psalm 76:4, NKJV).** Until we see God for who He is, we cannot effectively engage Him on the mountain of prayer. But the day on which the revelation of God's greatness dawns on our hearts is the day the morning star rises within our hearts. Our vocal cords will yield to God with praise songs declaring His majesty amongst the heathen. Christians who don't have this witness in their spirits are the ones who end up as prey on the mountains of challenges, tribulations, and setbacks in their sojourn on this side of heaven. This world's elemental and political powers can easily manipulate their lives. Yet, those convinced that God is worthy of their praise know how to enter God's gates with thanksgiving and His courts with praise (Psalm 100:4-5). They know the potent power of praise as a sacrifice offered to the God of creation who rules and reigns over all the earth.

In Psalm 65:1-2, David again speaks to us from His experience in Prayer. He declares, **"¹Praise is awaiting You, O God, in Zion; And to You the vow shall be performed. O You who hear prayer, ²to You all flesh will come" (NKJV).** Praise God! Our God is praiseworthy, and it's for this reason we turn to Him in prayer. Those who have embraced prayer culture live by the conviction that this praiseworthy God will not share His glory with anyone. They know that 'no flesh,' regardless of their size and weight, can stand in the ranking of God. They know that the king, the rich, the nobles, the strong, and the wise of this world are all flesh who rely on God for their survival. It is for this reason we pray. We embrace the discipline of engaging God in the deep waters of communion. We cringe from shallow Christian prayer praxis and take our journey deeper in Christ, who commands us to ask until our joy is complete (John 16:24).

The second reason we see in Psalm 18:3b is that David declares **"...I cried to the Lord, and I was saved from my enemies" (CEB).** What does this say about why we pray? We pray not just because God alone is worthy of our praise but also because He alone has the power to save us from all our enemies. The modern mind might say, "well, I don't have any known enemies, so I don't need to pray." Such thinking has become infected by every wind of doctrines and insulated from the spiritual realities in society. While we may not have physical enemies like David had, we have a common sworn enemy. This adversary is constantly hunting for our souls like Saul hunted for the life of David. Our sworn enemy has the liberty and the means to employ all it takes in his service of tracking down our souls. In case you are one such Christian who thinks you have no enemy, please listen to the counsel of Peter today from 1 Peter 5:8:

"Be sober, be vigilant, because your adversary the devil walks about like a roaring lion, seeking whom he may devour." (NKJV)

Is this clear enough? Any Christian who means business with God must take heed to this counsel. Any Christian who is in the service of God or who intends to truly serve God cannot do so without accepting this pill of truth. To think that you have no enemy proves that you've lost your spiritual sensitivity and vigilance. You have spent too much time interacting with the philosophies and ideas from humanism's limited scope. Doubting the devil's persistent monitoring of your soul to devour is to have been stripped of a vital spiritual diet and be laid bare in the open as prey for the evils of this world. Now, don't get me wrong, I am not advocating that you become conscious of devils and demons. What I say to you is to never ignore the warnings of Scripture about your soul. Remember that Peter is one of the Apostles of the Lamb. He knew what it meant to fail and deny the Lord under the pressure and potential of being crucified. Peter had learned the lesson of soberness when Satan came to sift him. We will do well to pay attention to what he has to say if we will not become preys, victims, and casualties in the hands of our arch adversary. It is for this reason we pray.

We pray because we are faced with many troubles and adversities crafted by the devil in this world. We're no match for this ancient serpent and stand no chance of victory except that the Lord helps us. So, we, too, must cry to God in prayer for help, acknowledging our helplessness. By so doing, God can put His strength upon us, and the weakest amongst us can fight like David and overcome, and those as strong as David like the angel of the Lord (Zechariah 12:8). Listen to how David describes God's strength in Psalm 18:31-34:

"³¹For who is God, except the Lord? And who is a rock, except our God? ³²It is God who arms me with strength,

and makes my way perfect. ³³He makes my feet like the feet of deer, and sets me on my high places. ³⁴He teaches my hands to make war, so that my arms can bend a bow of bronze." (NKJV)

I don't know about you, but I have concluded that I stand no chance of fulfilling my destiny without the strength that comes from God. For this reason, I pray, and we must pray for this reason. In a world where the rich rule over the poor and the powerful control the weak, prayer is the only way to overcome oppressive powers. We can escape becoming victims of adverse circumstances in life by hiding in the secret place of the Most High and abiding under the shadow of the Almighty through a lifestyle of prayer. In the contemplation of Asaph in Psalm 74:20, he cries **"Consider the covenant! Because the land's dark places are full of violence. Don't let the oppressed live in shame. No, let the poor and needy praise your name!" (CEB).**

Anyone who hopes to travel far in destiny and live above the oppressing forces on the earth must learn the ways of prayer. In a society bedeviled by systemic oppression, the only way to navigate life successfully is to journey under the strength of prayer and the mighty hands of God. And when you realize that you're constantly oppressed by forces higher than you, the sure way to escape from such a precarious state is to learn and embrace the culture of prayer. Someone might still be thinking in their heart saying, but I am 'not poor and needy.' To such, I say, hear these words again, **"We know that we are of God, and the whole world lies under the sway of the wicked one" (1John 5:19, NKJV).** Let it be clear in your heart that as long as you number amongst the earth's inhabitants, there is the possibility that the wicked one will come for you and hunt for your soul. And in the day that the wicked one comes knocking at your door, like Christ, Satan must find nothing of his in you (John 14:30). The winning way over evil forces is learning and leaning on the strength that Jehovah imparts into our spirits.

I ask again, why should you pray? We pray because our God is worthy of our praise, and when and whenever we call upon the name of the Lord, He shall save us. He shall deliver us from situations beyond our scope of wisdom and powers that defy the limits of the capacity of our strength. As believers in Christ, we all have our different ordinations from God, but we may never walk in them until we learn the way of prayer. We need to follow the example of David, who had to pray to escape Saul's attacks on his soul. David, who could have died though he was anointed to be king, fulfilled his divine ordination because he learned the way of prayer. So likewise, we must pray to escape from the forces of darkness and of this world that is constantly militating against our souls for us to fulfill our God-given ordinations. David could have died with all his gifts and the anointing of God upon him. But he escaped and lived to be the man God wanted him to be, not by his own strength but by the power that God supplied. No one can casually become all that God wants them to be, and no one who desires to be all that God wants them to be can do so without a lifestyle of prayer.

Those who do not see their need for prayer are bereft of understanding their God-given destiny in Christ. But those who know what God has ordained them to be and accomplish in their family, community, local church, and in the world today are rich. For David, he was anointed to become a king in Israel; For me, I know my calling is to be a husband, a father, and an apostle of the kingdom to the nations. So, I ask you, do you know what you have been called to do in this world? And how passionate are you about fulfilling your calling? This is why we pray. We pray so that no hellish power can circumvent our lives, waste our destinies, and reduce our glorious living in Christ to mere existence. We pray so that we are not swayed to abandon the pursuit of God for the search for the mundane things of this world. We pray so that our lives can serve God's purpose in our generation and show forth the excellency of our God and His Christ. We pray to become untouchable from the powers of oppression that rule the world. And we pray to triumph over all limitations-mental, emotional, financial, physical, or spiritual, which seek to keep us from finding and living out all that God has made us to be in Christ.

When we learn the ways of prayer, we can reach our goals and fulfill our destiny. We can escape from "destiny destroyers," be they the powers of poverty, the dangers of comfort, the complexities and failures of human relationships, or the world's grip that constantly seeks to conform us to its mold. If we learn the way of prayer, our lives will not be cut short, and we will not die before our time. Instead, we will walk in superior wisdom to navigate the complexities of life and know what to do in each season of our lives. For example, we pray so our children can escape the gun violence that is rampaging our society. We pray so our children can live to see their dreams come true. We call upon God's name so that our daughters can escape becoming victims of sexual abductions. We intercede in prayer so our young ones can escape the powers of addiction that rage in our society. When we build a culture that honors the call to prayer, there will be a supply of strength from God, and our anchor shall not fail on life's stormy sea. It means God Himself will be the covering of our defenseless heads in the days of battle. It means we can look forward to a good old age and leave a legacy of righteousness and great possibilities for our children and their children. When through obedience, we choose to do business with God in the deep waters of prayer, He will bless our water and our food. He will keep sicknesses and diseases away from our dwellings (Exodus 23:25).

CHAPTER TWO:

PRAYER, A SPIRITUAL EXERCISE

"⁴The pangs of death surrounded me, and floods of ungodliness made me afraid. ⁵The sorrows of Sheol surrounded me; The snares of death confronted me. ⁶In my distress I called upon the Lord, and cried out to my God; He heard my voice from His temple, and my cry came before Him, even to His ears."
(Psalm 18:4-6, NKJV)

To the undiscerning, prayer looks simple and seems like an activity that can be accomplished naturally. Yet, experience has shown that prayer is a spiritual exercise, and the results of prayer are equally spiritual before they become tangible. When you take a closer look at the situation David described in the text above, you'll discover that it takes energy whose source is beyond the natural to stand in the face of death. Without a doubt, life-threatening situations are the hardest to deal with. And in the case of David, some of the threats around his life came from the king himself. We saw earlier in 2 Samuel 22:1 that David's only named enemy was Saul, the insecure first king of Israel. Saul saw the exploit of David against Goliath as a threat to his reign. And with his life under constant malicious and vicious governmental surveillance, David knew from whence his help must come. So, calling upon the name of the Lord under such circumstances could not come naturally. It takes some measure of boldness and audacity not possessed by many to stay long in prayer until victory comes. How often do we tire out in the face of persistent and unrepentant challenges? How quickly do we look for other means of escape when we come under severe pressure instead of looking up to God?

Can you recall when you were confronted by a situation beyond your control? How did you fare? Perhaps you responded in one of these ways: First, you found strength in God to stay your ground until you received His help. Second, you became overwhelmed and sought help elsewhere. Third, you gave up and allowed the stormy situation to play out its natural course. As Christians, we sometimes give up in troubled times. While we know that God answers prayer, the energy and endurance needed in prayer are not always available. This is because praying is a natural activity that can only be propelled by supernatural strength. For example, it's much easier and more comfortable to binge-watch a movie series on Netflix or Amazon Prime and spend hours entertaining ourselves than binge-watching in prayer.' Try to recall the last time you were determined to pray; you'll remember how quickly your flesh administered the sleeping pill into your system and you dozed off until morning. Or try to gather a group of brethren for a day of fasting and prayer; you'll quickly realize that the most eloquent amongst the group has suddenly lost the speaking anointing. Such an outcome suggests that we need God's supply of strength to pray – and much more so in difficult times and under challenging circumstances.

Matthew 26:36-45 captures our weakness in the place of prayer. The text reveals that Jesus took three of His elite disciples to Gethsemane and said to them, **"My soul is exceedingly sorrowful, even to death. Stay here and watch with Me" (vs. 38, NKJV).** When their master shared such a burden with them, one would think that these disciples would be moved with compassion to stay with Him and pray. But not so. You would think that Peter, the most vocal of Jesus' disciples, would share in His sorrow and cry out to God in prayer with and for Him. But not so. None of them could watch, stay, and pray with Him. Three times Jesus came back to meet them after spending an hour in prayer and He found them sleeping. This experience is one of the rarest moments recorded in Scripture where Christ expressed surprise. And here is how He expressed His dismay: **"What? Could you not watch with Me one hour?" "Are you still sleeping and resting?" (vs. 40b and 45b, NKJV).** We can only imagine the shock Jesus felt, seeing that His disciples couldn't stay with Him in prayer for an hour, let alone three hours, when His soul was overwhelmed with sorrow. But if you've ever been disappointed, you know what that looks and feels like. Instead of watching and praying, these disciples were sleeping and resting. We must learn from Christ's experience that in life, we must not be totally dependent on people, but on God. Knowing this must stir our hearts to build a reliable prayer life with God, who is our very help in times of need.

Let's bring this home with a question: how often do you pray, and how much time do you spend in prayer? How long has it been since you stayed with the Lord in prayer for an hour? How about three hours? Do you make prayer your first priority, or you are comfortable giving God the leftover of your time? The path to liberation is to answer this question as honestly as possible. By so doing, it will be easy to move the hands of God for the supply of strength we need to become Christians who are watchers in prayer. By coming to Him as we are, we can find a lifeline that the weakness of the flesh cannot overcome so that the will of God can prosper in our lives. If God opens your eyes and gives you access to His heart, you will find that the same burden in Jesus' heart while at Gethsemane is still God's burden today. God's still concerned about the unsaved for whom Jesus died. He's still looking for believers who lift their voices in prayer to break the powers of darkness over the nations. God's still searching and waiting for believers who will become the bridge between Him and the unsaved. The fact that some are yet to appropriate Christ's great sacrifice in their standing with God is a burden God wants to share with us. So, we must wake up from our slumber and be the ones that God can rely on and confide in to bring many more people into the saving knowledge of Christ.

The excuse for not watching and praying hasn't changed much. It's how we are arguing for those excuses that have gotten better. For Peter and the sons of Zebedee, their excuse was their need for sleep and rest; It's still the same for us today. We have time for all other things except prayer. We're more inclined to make exceptions and sacrifices for other things than we are to watch and pray. Look no further if you're reading this and wondering why your spiritual growth has been truncated or plateauing. Every spiritual apathy is traceable to the culture of prayerlessness. Today, many Christians justify their absence from the place and time of prayer by citing their work schedule and other activities. When we have spent most of our time and energy doing other things (including work and career development), we conclude and justify our need for sleep and rest. We convince ourselves that God understands. In this way, the fire of prayer on our altar gradually dies out. Some of us still try to pray to have some religious satisfaction. We spend a few minutes in prayer and go about our daily business. No wonder our prayers are void of power, and the name of Jesus in our mouths does not carry much authority.

Listen to me: Christ has a sharp rebuke for us this season. When His disciples continued to sleep and rest when they should have been watching and praying, He said to them; **"Keep alert and pray. Otherwise temptation will overpower you" (Matt. 26:41a, The Living Bible).** Now, that's a warning every serious believer must internalize. If we fail to stay alert and stay with Christ in prayer, if we keep sleeping and resting, then, when temptation comes, we may have no reserved power to stand. And on that day, when temptations come, every other thing we have tried to build stands the risk of becoming overpowered by the forces that drive such temptations. When those we rely on for help fails us, we may find it too difficult to heal from such disappointment, forgive, and move forward with the strength that only God supplies.

Further, it's expedient for us to know that Satan often disguises when he comes to tempt us. The enemy of our soul is not in the habit of announcing his arrival. The Message Translation of Matthew 26:41a best captures the subtlety of temptation. It says, **"Stay alert; be in prayer so you don't wander into temptation without even knowing you're in danger."** Do you see that? We can escape danger if we know it's coming. We can avoid untimely death (spiritual or physical) and the fowler's snare if we have the proper spiritual skill set. Yet, many have wandered off into temptations without knowing what hits them. So likewise, some believers today have wandered into apostasy without knowing it. While they still have the forms and rituals of religion, they have been shifted away from the desire to lay hold of the presence and power of God. Unfortunately, Satan will not stop us from our preoccupation with religious activities. He will not prevent us from using church jargon in our lingo, but he is fiercest at keeping us from praying.

The challenge we face in acquiring a suitable spiritual skill set happens to be the prerequisite to overcoming the perils of life. Staying alert and staying in prayer are two sides of the same coin we need to fight off temptations and be ready for troubled times. From Christ's perspective, staying alert and praying are not mere suggestions; they are commandments we need to obey. The answer to slumbering off in prayer is prayer; the solution to the possibility of getting overpowered by temptation is prayer. The way to prayer is not in doing Bible Study on prayer without praying. To pray requires taking action, and that action is intentionally developing the consecration of calling upon the name of the Lord.

Friends, with your lack of time, or little time for daily prayer, you cannot do much for yourself and the people you love. We must not even conceive the idea of accomplishing much for God outside of the practice of consistent prayer. E.M. Bounds said, "What the Church needs today is not more machinery or better organizations or more novel methods, but men whom the Holy Ghost can use–men of prayer, men mighty in prayer."[4] If we hope not to transfer a powerless religion to our children, we must follow the command to stay alert and pray. Let me remind you that the day to start learning how to use the sword is not the day of battle. Anyone who waits until the tempter comes has only one possibility left: they will fail and fall head-on into temptation except by an act of divine mercy. The only thing that awaits a Christian who waits until troubles come before flexing their spiritual muscles is to stand the risk of being overpowered.

The measure of our Christian strength is validated not in times of comfort and pleasure but in moments of distress and strain. Don't take my words for it; Proverbs 24:10 speaks directly about it. Let's look at it from a few versions:

"Don't give up and be helpless in times of trouble" (CEV)

"If you grow weary when times are troubled, your strength is limited" (ISV)

"If you faint in the day of adversity, your strength is small" (NKJV)

"If you show yourself lacking courage on the day of distress, your strength is meager" (ASB)

"If you do nothing in a difficult time, your strength is limited" (HCSB)

"If you slack (careless) in the day of distress, your strength is limited" (Amp)

"If you fall to pieces in a crisis, there wasn't much to you in the first place" (The Message)

Child of God, the best time to demonstrate the strength of God within our spirit is on the day of battle. The best day for God's superior wisdom to reign is when we find ourselves in a confusing circumstance. The days of trouble, weakness, and distress are the glory days of the saints because that's when God wants to show Himself strong. During Jesus' earthly ministry, the disciples would have missed the opportunity to know He had the power to speak to the wind, the wave, and the sea until they found themselves in the middle of the storm, and Christ rebuked it. Their exclamation was, **"What kind of a man is this, that even the winds and the sea obey Him" (Matt. 8:27, NASB).** The mark of our spiritual strength and status must be fully displayed when we come under pressure and the times are troubled. What we call storms of life, setbacks, delays, challenges, sicknesses, diseases, poverty, barrenness, stagnations, and dealing with the problem of evil in the world today are opportunities for God to demonstrate His power. God desires to manifest His glory in our lives so that we and those around us can still exclaim, **"What manner of God is this that even the chaos of life still obey Him!"**

In the case of David, the reason he found strength when the pangs of death surrounded him is that he bore witness that the Lord was his rock. He lived convinced that God was his strength, fortress, shield, and the horn of his salvation before the day of troubles came. God had taught David's hands to war and his arms to bend the bow of bronze before his enemies came against him like a flood. In Psalm 18:18, David testified that **"They confronted me in the day of my calamity, but the Lord was my support" (NKJV).** It's not surprising that we have been called to fight the good fight of faith. As such, we don't have to be swept away by the tides of troubled times. We don't have to give in under pressure, nor do we have to bow the knee to devils. We have to be unafraid of facing the consequences of standing for God and bearing His light amidst the darkness of this age. Believers who have learned the way of prayer know that if they don't bow to pressure, they will not burn and will not be overpowered by temptations. Weakness in the face of distress can be replaced by the strength that the Holy Spirit supplies. The limitations that drown others don't have to drown us. We can exercise authority over difficult times and arrest the evil that drives the hellish vices we see around our lives. This is the will of God for His saints; it is our destiny to show forth the glory of the Lord, as the prophet Isaiah describes it in Isaiah 60:1-2:

"¹Arise Jerusalem, and shine like the sun; The glory of the LORD is shining on you! ²Other nations will be covered by darkness, But on you the light of the Lord will shine; The brightness of his presence will be with you." (GNT)

It is time to arise and shine in glory by putting temptations under our feet and disarming the weapons fashioned against our lives, families, local churches, and communities. If you're going through troubled times, know that there is help for you, and you can rise again. But we will not find answers in our own strength unless we want to fall again as quickly as we rise. We cannot thrive when darkness covers the earth by shining our own light. Therefore, anyone who hopes to arise must choose to become a watcher in the place of prayer. Such individuals must come to the same conclusion as Christ in Matthew 26:41b. He said to His disciples, **"For the spirit indeed is willing, but how weak the body is!" (Matt. 26:41b, TLB).**

I remember telling myself in December of 2001 that I was going to go on a spiritual adventure to fast and pray for three days without taking food or water. I wanted to do this not because I was under pressure, nor was I surrounded by an overwhelmingly difficult circumstance, as in the case of David. Instead, I wanted to show the Lord that I loved Him and wanted to seek Him like I had never done before. I pursued this intent by booking a room on a Christian campsite away from home, packed my bag, and took off on this spiritual escapade. It didn't take long to learn the lesson Jesus taught His disciples on the willingness of the spirit and the weakness of the flesh. When I arrived at the campsite gate, I saw folks selling loaves of sliced bread. And oh my, those loves smelled so good! That was the end of my zeal for dry fasting; my determination was highjacked by the smell of fresh-baked bread.

Nevertheless, I reckoned that I could still observe praying with adjusted fasting of living on bread and peanut butter. So, I continued with my mutilated plan and thanked God for His mercies; He still allowed me access into His presence. That experience is one of the spiritual pillars of my life, marriage, and ministry today. I know by experience that except the Lord helps us, our prayer altars will run out of fire. While our spirit is always willing to pray, the willingness we feel within will not always translate to action.

Experienced men have taught us that we cannot go far with God in prayer by our own strength. For example, Martin Luther, the great reformer, wrote in 1529, in his hymn **"A Mighty Fortress Is Our God,"**[5]

"Did we in our own strength confide,

Our striving would be losing.

Were not the right man on our side,

The man of God's own choosing.

Dost ask who that may be?

Christ Jesus, it is he;

Lord Sabaoth, his name, from age to age the same,

And he must win the battle."

Praise God that there's a provision for our flesh's weaknesses, limitations, and infirmities in Christ. His provision for our deliverance from prayerlessness and the overpowering powers of temptation is captured in Zechariah 12:8-10a:

"⁸In that day the Lord will defend the inhabitants of Jerusalem; the one who is feeble among them in that day shall be like David, and the house of David shall be like God, like the Angel of the Lord before them. ⁹It shall be in that day that I will seek to destroy all the nations that come against Jerusalem. ¹⁰And I will pour on the house of David and on the inhabitants of Jerusalem the Spirit of grace and supplication; Then they will look on Me whom they pierced." (NKJV).

Glory! God has made a provision for our defense and deliverance, and that provision is by furnishing us with His Spirit. God has chosen to garnish us with prayer strength through the supply of the Spirit of grace and supplication. This speaks of the capacity that is in the Holy Spirit that makes grace available whenever we want to pray. He comes to anoint our hearts, so our willingness to pray outshines the weakness of the flesh. He comes to think through us and speak through us so we can know what to pray and how to pray (Romans 8:26-27). So, if we can ask God to pour His Holy Spirit upon us, we can pray and pray through. If we can recognize that we are weak, but He is strong, He can quicken us so we can expend His energy to pray and not burn out. A revival will find its way into our spirit that can energize us with the ability to commune with God and enjoy the glory and brightness of His presence. And whereas we have been looking upon other things for help, the Holy Spirit can refocus our gaze. We can look on Him that was pierced for our iniquity; **"The author and finisher of our faith" (Heb. 12:2).** It means the weight that weakens us can become the wind that lifts us into the very presence of God, where we can find proper rest for our weary souls.

Hear me: we are not as defenseless as Satan wants us to think. God has made it plain that our defense and deliverance from all the hellish forces of this world are in our redemption package. So, the day of protection and help is here, and the dangers surrounding us will no longer bother us. The destructions that fly in the noonday will no longer come near our dwellings. All the vicious attacks from the forces of hell will be in vain against you and yours if you can cry out to God for the outpouring of His Spirit of grace and supplication. So, if there's any cry to loudly vocalize today, it is for power enduement. It is not the lament of how poor, needy, and bedeviled by sicknesses and diseases we are but a cry for the supply of God's Spirit. None of us should henceforth be feeble nor be a weakling in the battle against the kingdom of darkness and violence that lurks in the dark places of the earth. God's promise is that by the Spirit of grace and supplication, **"The one who is feeble among them in that day shall be like David, and the house of David shall be like God, like the Angel of the Lord before them."** It's clear God wants me to be strong, and God wants you to be mighty. God wants us to be as strong as an angel –that by the in-working of the Spirit of grace and supplication within us, God can have Himself an army who knows how to conquer on their knees.

The day of salvation is here! This is the time to be strong and take the battle to the enemy's gates. God wants to raise an army of Christ's soldiers trained to be strong and weather any storm and push back the forces of darkness. I have a question for you: Do you want to be numbered in this army? Do you want to be made strong? If your answer is yes, then it is time to pray and cry that the Holy Spirit will come upon you, and the presence and power of God will break open within your heart. It takes the power of the Holy Spirit to receive Christ's victory over sin, sickness, diseases, and the endless circle of negative occurrences in our lives. We must look upon Him that was pierced, and the Holy Spirit has come to make sure we can do so. The next level of your spiritual growth and service will not be possible without the prayer power that comes from the Holy Spirit. But when the Spirit of grace and supplication finds expression in your heart, your defense will be sure, and you will no longer be weak. You will be empowered to live a flourishing life and fulfill your God-given destiny.

I hope you can sense the nudge to pray. If you do, I want you to pray. Pray; don't wait. Pray now and follow the cry that rises within your spirit. William Walford penned these words in 1845 in **"Sweet Hour of Prayer"**[6]: [Perhaps you would like to sing it if you're familiar with the song and confess it if you're unfamiliar with it]:

1. Sweet hour of prayer!
   Sweet hour of prayer!
   That calls me from a world of care,
   And bids me at my Father's throne
   Make all my wants and wishes known.
   In seasons of distress and grief,
   My soul has often found relief,
   And often escaped the tempter's snare
   By thy return, sweet hour of prayer!
2. Sweet hour of prayer!
   Sweet hour of prayer!

The joys I feel, the bliss I share
Of those whose anxious spirits burn
With strong desires for thy return!
With such I hasten to the place
Where God my Savior shows his face,
And gladly take my station there,
And wait for thee, sweet hour of prayer!

3. Sweet hour of prayer!
Sweet hour of prayer!
Thy wings shall my petition bear
To him whose truth and faithfulness
Engage the waiting soul to bless.
And since he bids me seek his face,
Believe his word, and trust his grace,
I'll cast on him my every care,
And wait for thee, sweet hour of prayer!

Go to the Lord in prayer and in the next chapter, I'll be talking about the length of prayer. So read on and let this revival be fully established in your heart.

Chapter Three:

OF PRAYER LENGTH

"Then David spoke to the LORD the words of this song, on the day when the Lord had delivered him from the hand of all his enemies, and from the hand of Saul." (2Samuel 22:1, NKJV)

I n this chapter, I would like to share about prayer length. Let's find out how long we can pray over a matter before we give up on it? One of the discouraging factors in prayer is a delay, the frustration we experience when we don't see tangible results of what we pray about when we want it. Many people want to pray, and some do pray. However, whenever it seems our desired outcome is taking longer than expected, we lose the courage to continue in prayer. This is where pessimism steps in, and doubt is allowed to take over our hearts. The prayer life of many Christians today would have become life-dispensing machinery in God's hands only if they had answered the question of prayer length. Many believers have justified why they quit praying with the words of Solomon in Proverbs 13:12a, which says, **"Hope deferred makes the heart sick."** The challenge with using this Scripture to justify the weariness that leads to abandoning prayer is that we don't always remember to quote part 'b' of the text. I will say more on this later.

Whenever we accept discouragement, we give an in-way for confusion, settle for the average, and pat ourselves on the back. We then wallow in self-pity and embrace a mediocre Christian life where God seems far away each time it hurts. When we feel our needs the most, we seek help in places where there is none. This experience makes some folks drawback in their service to God and gradually walk away from believers' gatherings in the local church. Some believers might even cut down on their giving to God and resort to a casual commitment to God and His kingdom. Don't get me wrong, in the battle called life, no one is a superman except the ones the Lord has helped. However, if we believe God's word is still relevant, we must remind ourselves that the Scriptures teach that we are more than conquerors. Romans 8:31-39 is worth reading aloud to yourself: **"[31]What then shall we say to these things? If God is for us, who can be against us? [32]He who did not spare His own Son, but delivered Him up for us all, how shall He not with Him also freely give us all things? [33]Who shall bring a charge against God's elect? It is God who justifies. [34]Who is he who condemns? It is Christ who died, and furthermore is**

also risen, who is even at the right hand of God, who also makes intercession for us. ³⁵Who shall separate us from the love of Christ? Shall tribulation, or distress, or persecution, or famine, or nakedness, or peril, or sword? ³⁶As it is written: "For Your sake we are killed all day long; We are accounted as sheep for the slaughter." ³⁷Yet in all these things we are more than conquerors through Him who loved us. ³⁸For I am persuaded that neither death nor life, ³⁹nor angels nor principalities nor powers, nor things present nor things to come, nor height nor depth, nor any other created thing, shall be able to separate us from the love of God which is in Christ Jesus our Lord." (NKJV)

Prevailing prayers don't just happen; people make them happen. To see God's hand move powerfully on our behalf, we need the persuasion the text above speaks about to stay with God in prayer until our joy is complete. And until we start approaching God knowing that nothing can separate us from Him, our prayers cannot avail much. Prayer power can only be experienced within the crucible of reposing complete and absolute confidence in God. When we come to Him as unto the One who answers prayer, that's when we lay hold of the more than conqueror's realm. The doctrinal knowledge that describes Christians as overcomers become our experiential knowledge. When we engage God with the determination that nothing and no one is good enough to separate us from Him, we transition into the league of those who fight the good fight of faith and prevail. When this foundation is not well established in our hearts, we will be strangers to the supernatural dimensions of God and its manifestations in our lives. Believers who have power with God live daily with the conviction that no height nor depth, angels nor principalities nor powers, things known nor things unknown can separate them from the love of God.

The earthly foundation upon which God's power is released is a self-abandoned heart before the Lord. Those who meet this prerequisite are watchers, not of time, but of the signs that the Spirit of Christ within them will impress upon their hearts. People who will see the supernatural manifestation of God's power over what they pray for are the ones the Scripture describes as **"Whoever believes will not act hastily."** The reason this stock of Christians will not make haste is enclosed in the full text of Isaiah 28:16. It says, **"Therefore thus says the Lord: I lay in Zion a stone for a foundation, a tried stone, a precious cornerstone, a sure foundation: Whoever believes will not act hastily" (NKJV).** It means we need to allow God to take us through His refining process where He moves us from being a stone to a tried stone, one that can stand the test of time and withstand the pressures of the elements. As we give God this allowance, He keeps working on our lives until we become precious stones in His hands. Many believers can confess that they are the apple of God's eye (Deut. 32:10), but only a few know what this means by experience. And such experiential knowledge is reserved for those in the business of building intimacy with God. Those who have taken such a yoke upon themselves are the ones who can become a sure cornerstone. Their faith in God is unshakable. They are the believers who have overcome the dangers and limitations of haste in their communion with God.

When next you are discouraged in prayer and are tempted to say hope deferred makes the heart sick, remember that God has bigger dreams for you. Proverbs 13:12 says, **"Hope deferred makes the heart sick. But when the desire comes, it is a tree of life" (Proverbs 13:12, NKJV).** Tell yourself that God's ultimate intention is to plant a tree in your heart. The tree that will become a life-dispensing power and those who eat its fruit will never remain the same. Every one of us must be determined in deciding what kind of a Christian we want to be. If we are the salt and light of the world, we can't accomplish much for God if we are in the habit of quitting much in the place of prayer. We will do well to constantly remind ourselves that God's time is never our time.

David's life and His testimony offer us a veritable example of what it means to fight the good fight of faith until we receive a response from God. Take a look again at 2 Samuel 22:1, **"Then David spoke to the LORD the words of this song, on the day when the Lord had delivered him from the hand of all his enemies, and from the hand of Saul" (NKJV).** A casual look at the text can stir the tendency to think that the testimony David spoke about in the rest of the chapter happened in a day. Because the Scripture says, **"On the day when the Lord delivered him…,"** many may think the deliverance occurred overnight. However, we know from the Scripture that David was a young man when he entered the service of Saul. So, the David speaking here was an old man who has advanced in years and experience. The deliverance David spoke about here took place over many years. His enemies were many, and Saul happened to be the first amongst David's numerous enemies. However, it will do us good to take a quick view of the enmity David suffered from Saul for the subject at hand. The woes and aches of David began after he killed Goliath and the news of His exploit went across the land. Here is how the Bible describes it in 1 Samuel 18:7-12: **"⁷So the women sang as they danced, and said: "Saul has slain his thousands, and David his ten thousands." ⁸Then Saul was very angry, and the saying displeased him; and he said, "They have ascribed to David ten thousands, and to me they have ascribed only thousands. Now what more can he have but the kingdom?" ⁹So Saul eyed David from that day forward. ¹⁰And it happened on the next day that the distressing spirit from God came upon Saul, and he prophesied inside the house. So David played music with his hand, as at other times; but there was a spear in Saul's hand. ¹¹And Saul cast the spear, for he said, "I will pin David to the wall!" But David escaped his presence twice.**

¹²Now Saul was afraid of David, because the LORD was with him, but had departed from Saul" (NKJV).

The above Scripture describes how the state-sponsored oppression of David began, and with it, so also began David's cry unto God for deliverance. David was persecuted, misrepresented, and became a fugitive from this time on. At some point, he had to flee and seek refuge in the house of his enemy, the king of Gath, which is the home of the slain Goliath (1 Samuel 21). At Gath, David was so afraid of his life that the Bible says, **"So he changed his behavior before them, pretended madness in their hands, scratched on the doors of the gate, and let his saliva fall down on his beard" (1 Samuel 21:13, NKJV).** It was that dire and threatening. As we imagine what life must have looked like for David at this time, we must remember that his prayer for deliverance had already begun. So, it's safe to say that David's decision to feign madness was an inspired decision. This precarious situation with Saul stayed until Saul died in battle, and David was crowned king at thirty (2 Samuel 2). So, when the Bible says David spoke a song unto God, **"On the day the Lord delivered him from His enemies and from the hand of Saul,"** the deliverance from Saul alone took about 10 years. David's cry for deliverance from Saul wasn't a one-time cry. It was a consistent cry that spanned about a decade.

One thing is clear from David's experience; His testimony was birthed by cries for help. You just need to read through the Psalms to see what spiritual warfare looked like for David. In Psalm 27:13-14, David gives us an insight into his tenacious prayer life and how he stood by his faith in God. It says, **"¹³I would have lost heart, unless I had believed that I would see the goodness of the Lord in the land of the living. ¹⁴Wait on the Lord; Be of good courage, and He shall strengthen your heart; Wait, I say, on the Lord!" (NKJV).** Such is the heart and determination of men who prevailed in prayer. When opportunities presented themselves for him to lose heart, the belief system he had built became his sustenance and anchor. When he had all the right reasons to compromise his stand, David remembered that God's promises were unfailing. He knew that unchanging are God's promises and faithful is He who has promised him, for He will bring His promises to pass. For believers of this stock, when the world comes at them to entice them with lovely goodies, they remember God has a special kind of goodness called **"the goodness of the Lord"** with their names on it. They are confident in experiencing God's goodness not in the land of the dead but in the land of the living. They know that God is neither too late nor too early to save them. This caliber of believers functions from a different perspective, which could make them seek refuge in their enemy's home, if need be, without an iota of doubts about God's ability to save them. Christians who live like this know that God's leading is their commandment and that if need be, they must obey God, being afraid. These are the ones who are constantly building the skills of working out their salvation with fear and trembling.

So, here's the time tried and tested wisdom we can buy from David; **"Wait on the Lord; Be of good courage, and He shall strengthen your heart; Wait, I say, on the Lord!"** (**Ps. 27:14, NKJV**). You'll agree that David is qualified to bring us such command based on his many years of travails, trials, and triumphs. For this, we will do well to harken to a warrior's command, challenging us to wait on the Lord and be of good courage. And as if he could hear our push back on that command, he reiterated, **"Wait, I say, on the Lord!"** With that our innocence has been bought. We are no longer ignorant of how God wants to work in us, so we too can become kingdom warriors who will work the works of God and fight the Lord's battle against the kingdom of darkness. The question we need to start asking now is the processing question: What does it mean to wait on the Lord? Our ability to extract the meat from that instruction will become our initiation into the league of warriors who can accomplish much for God through prayer. So, we need to search out what it means to wait on the Lord, lest we become guilty of assumption.

Waiting on the Lord is not a call to idleness but a command to take a posture before the Lord with the readiness to receive and execute divine directives. I found Campbell G. Morgan's inspired words on what it means to wait enlightening. He said, "Waiting for God is not laziness. Waiting for God is not going to sleep. Waiting for

God is not abandonment of effort. Waiting for God means, first, activity under command; Second, readiness for any new command that may come; Third, the ability to do nothing until the command is given."[7] How insightful! It's expedient to have clarity of mind and purpose as we journey with God through prayer. Some have erroneously concluded that praying long and waiting long in God's presence is laziness. And there are believers today who spend long hours asking God for frivolous things– for mundane reasons. They have abandoned their position of waiting, which makes for their liberation. Satan has found a way of robbing us of an eternal principle that he knows would wreck his kingdom. Waiting upon the Lord is standing our watch with great expectancy to hear what the Lord has to say to us. The calmness comes with an assurance that we know God has something to tell us when we approach Him in prayer. Waiting upon the Lord is the balance between working and praying. It is a posture in God that, on the one hand, shows our absolute reliance on God and, on the other hand, reveals our ability to do nothing until the Lord says so.

Waiting upon the Lord is a prophetic posture that clarifies our destiny in life. It grants us the ability to make sure steps that will secure God's provisions for our lives. Here is how Habakkuk the prophet explains it: **"[1]I will stand my watch and set myself on the rampart, and watch to see what He will say to me, and what I will answer when I am corrected. [2]Then the Lord answered me and** said: Write the vision and make it plain on tablets, that he may run who reads it. ³For the vision is yet for an appointed time; But at the end it will speak, and it will not lie. Though it tarries, wait for it: Because it will surely come, it will not tarry. ⁴Behold the proud, his soul is not upright in him; But the just shall live by his faith." (Habakkuk 2:1-4, NKJV)

The above Scripture is fraught with gems of wisdom for God-seekers. If we want our lives to count on what truly matters and labor for that which will not perish, then the path of waiting is unavoidable. Habakkuk had cried to God in the first chapter about the violence in the land. In fact, in his case, he had called for a long time, and it looked as if God's ears were blocked. He had told God, **"O Lord, how long shall I cry, and You will not hear? Even cry out to You, "Violence!" And You will not save" (Hab. 1:2, NKJV).** Yet, he did not stop crying out to God and pouring out his heart for another fifteen verses. Whatever tells you to stop crying out to God because you didn't receive your answer when you want it is the devil's voice. Wise spiritual people know that God will answer, and that's why they stay in prayer until He responds. Waiting is what we do when we have prayed and God did not answer. It is the place where God corrects our motives and refines our hearts. Waiting is where our prayers go through God's refinery so we can pray the things in His heart instead of praying the items on our hearts. So, Habakkuk tells us, **"I will stand my watch and set myself on the rampart,**

and watch to see what He will say to me, and what I will answer when I am corrected."

I don't know what violence you see around you that has brought you to the place of prayer. I don't know what degree of oppression, physical, emotional, financial, or spiritual, for which you're calling upon the Lord. Yours may be frustration in your professional life, marriage, or even parenting, and you're wondering, "How much longer, Lord? When will this pain end? When will this vicious circle end?" You may have struggled with loneliness and childlessness without a spouse or a job. You may be saying to God, "When will you bring the right people into my life or give me my own family?" "Yours may be a violence in your health, a disease that's been cutting lives short in the family," and you're saying, "End it, Lord, end it, Lord!" Yet, it looks as if the more you pray, the more it hurts, and now you want to quit praying. Are you going through any frustration now that you're contemplating taking your own life? Let the word of the Lord come to you today: **WAIT ON THE LORD AND BE OF GOOD COURAGE, AND HE SHALL STRENGTHEN YOUR HEART!** Maybe you're reading this and have been frustrated in your business, career, or even ministry. You've been told righteousness is the narrow path of fulfillment, but that's not been working for you. Now you're tempted to try what others do to 'make it.' Can you stop to think and consider your ways? Stay with God! Stay with Him in prayer! He still has the package of goodness for you in the land of the living. Wait!

By waiting, God furnishes our heart with a heavenly vision, and it is with such vision we run. Until we have waited upon the Lord, we cannot access the knowledge of those things God has ordained for our lives and over our concerns at their appointed time. This is where true biblical faith is born. The only people who can't wait are the proud and the impatient. Hastiness and pride are first and foremost things that are rooted in the heart before they become a show of the flesh. Proud people don't wait for God; they always have other means of taking care of their concerns. Impatient people are comfortable believing that anything is better than nothing. If you're a Christian and you've never had a situation where the only solution you need can only be found in God, beware! Your life may be out of sync with heaven. If you're a Christian and you've become used to settling down for anything, it's an indication that you may never know the best of God for your life. But not so with the just. They are the ones who live by faith, by the proceeding words from the mouth of God. Waiting upon the Lord is the hobby of the righteous. They have come to see their need for God, and they know that they can do nothing without Him. Waiting is where our hearts are garnished with the strength we need to run and not be tired and to walk and not be wearied. The reason is that a heavenly vision has come into our hearts. And like the eagle soars towards the sun, we've glided towards the

Sun of righteousness, and we have received the healing powers of His wings!

Listen, friends, waiting upon the Lord is to cease from our fruitless labor until our steps in life are ordered by the Lord. It is our sure winning ways and our means of escaping dangers. When we wait upon the Lord, we're challenging His integrity to commit Himself to do what He has promised to do in us, for us, and through us. I know this might be too much risk for some folks because they can't imagine doing such things as challenging God. So, let me share a real-life story with you from several experiences about how God rewards the soul that waits upon Him and knows how to take Him by His word.

Four years ago, I was an international seminary student at Emory University's Candler School of Theology, Atlanta, Georgia. I was in my finals and looking forward to how God will be guiding my steps into ministry according to His words. But six months to graduation, all my inflow of cash stopped. The department I was working at in school was closed. And those who were sponsoring me could no longer do so due to astronomical heights of inflation in my home country, Nigeria. At this time, tuition was no longer an issue, as God had sorted that out miraculously. Yet, I was confronted by a situation that could have rendered my family and me homeless in Georgia. With no family in America and not having the privilege of building sufficient relational support in the United States, I had no options. We were strangers in the land. My wife and I prayed and spoke with the few people we knew, but no one could help. So, we kept praying; the more we prayed, the more roadblocks we met. After praying for four months, things finally got to the edge when I could no longer pay our rent. And after owing rent for two months, notifications began pouring in from my landlord asking for the rent and making sure I was aware of what the consequences could be. If I failed to pay up the two months' rent, we would run out of favor with her, and eviction would have become inevitable. And that's precisely what happened.

I was preparing for my finals and writing my final papers with this heavy burden on my heart. Yet, my wife and I kept praying and trusting that God would come through again as He has always done. But it was tough on me this time. I had my wife and our three little boys with me, and it became more challenging to practice faith. I said to the Lord at one time, "If I was by myself, You know I could go through this, but how exactly do I move forward with my family?" You might think that would have deployed an angel from heaven to help before we ran out of time but no. Finally, after praying and trusting the Lord for six months, the day came that the landlord and I had to meet for the last time on the matter. The conclusion was that we had to leave the apartment. My dilemma and perplexity were that I didn't know what to do or where to move my family to. On our way home from the meeting with the landlord, about 2.5 miles from the house, I told our neighbor who was driving us home to drop me by the roadside and go-ahead to take my wife and kids home. Now that I have been confronted with the possibility of becoming homeless in the United States, the burden in my heart has reached its fullest and heaviest.

So, I got out of the car. It was a quiet neighborhood, so I could scream my heart off as I walked home. So, I prayed, cried, spoke in understanding, and spoke in tongues. I reminded God that the idea of leaving Nigeria for the United States was not mine but His. I also reminded Him of His faithful provisions for our needs that have led me to that moment. Yet, I asked Him, "How could You bring me here and make way for my wife and children to join me only to be sending us homeless on the streets." Oh, I cried and prayed! I had moments of silence with tears running down my face. But then, from deep down in my spirit, the refreshing voice of God, like the evening breeze, spoke softly in my heart; "Praise me. When you get home, Praise me!" It took some thirty minutes or so to walk home. That was the longest walk I have ever done, not because of its length but because of the state of my heart.

When I got home, my wife wasn't sure what to say to me, but she cared, and I am forever grateful for her presence in my life. So, I said to her, the Lord said we should praise Him. That's how we came together as a family and shouted 50 hallelujahs to the Lord. And with that, we started getting ready to leave the apartment without knowing where we were going. We had just three days to pack before the landlord was to come for the keys. After our first day of packing, the Holy Spirit came again and said I should call one of my friends and that he would help me. So, I did and told him we needed a place to stay for two weeks. The other thing was that I had a job prospect with a United Methodist Conference in Minnesota. I had had an interview with their cabinet two months prior, and I was under the impression that an appointment was underway. So, I called my friend, and his response was that he would speak with his church to see if they would allow us to stay at their parsonage. The church had a parsonage that was not in use, and the next hurdle was to convince the leadership of the church to grant permission for us to use it for two weeks. We'll need to wait until my friend meets with his church leaders, and they were not meeting until the day I was to turn in our apartment's keys to my landlord.

So, we were packed, and keys were turned over to the landlord. We had to discard some of the little stuff we had because there was no way we could move around with that much stuff. I spoke with my neighbor to allow my wife and the kids to sleep over in their house the night we moved out. I would spend the night at my friend's house and await the church's decision later the following day. I remember telling my friend to be at peace as he was preparing for the leadership meeting at his church, where he planned to make a request for us. In the end, the church did not grant permission for us to move into their parsonage. They instead paid for a two-week stay for us at a hotel and even gave us gift cards for food. And within those two weeks, and with the church's help, an apartment was open for us through an agency that, two days earlier, had no available openings. So, we moved in and stayed rent-free for a year until God launched us into our next season of ministry. Praise the Lord!

I have shared my experience to encourage you in your own journey with God and whatever situation you may be going through. People who wait upon the Lord must know that they must stay in prayer until they hear from God. They know that, like Habakkuk, violence may surround them all around, but they must stand their watch and set themselves on the rampart, waiting to see what God will say to them. This stock of believers knows that God may not stop an army from pursuing them while He leads them in the direction of the Red Sea. Yet, they know that in those dilemmas, they will see God's glory in the land of the living; they know that if He parted the Red Sea before, He could do it again. They know that there's no other way of living outside of faith. Oppressive powers around them might increase the intensity of their oppression. Still, they have chosen never to bow to any authority that's not the God who made the heavens and the earth.

Hear the good news today; **"Cast your burden on the Lord, and He shall sustain you. He shall never permit the righteous to be moved" (Psalm 55:22, NKJV).** Stay in prayer. Cast your burdens upon Him. Keep casting your burdens upon Him. Do it for as long as the burdens remain. Cast it off until your heart is light and until you hear His whispers in your heart. At that moment, faith is born, and you can then praise Him until faith becomes sight. The God of the Bible is the Living and Compassionate God. He is the Friend of the poor and needy, Helper of the helpless, and the Defender of the defenseless. God's the One who says, **"Call to Me, and I will answer you, and show you great and mighty things, which you do not know (Jeremiah 33:3, NKJV).** He yet awaits your call. Take Him at His word and call on Him. He has great and mighty things to show you. Call on Him and tell Him those things that ache you and wait to see what He will say to you and what He has to show you. The things God shows you are the things He will do in You, with You, and for You; The things He reveals to you and the signs that He will yet glorify Himself in your life and through your situation. In the next chapter, I'll show you how "You Can Have What You Ask For." For now, it's time to pray. I encourage you to listen to your heart and find the song your heart is singing. Let that song be your transport into prayer.

Chapter Four:

YOU CAN HAVE
WHAT YOU ASK FOR

**"In my distress I called upon the Lord, and cried
out to my God; He heard my voice from His temple,
and my cry came before Him, and even to His ears."
(Psalm 18:6, NKJV)**

One of the deficiencies in our Christian experience today is that many believers know that God's promises in the Scripture are true, but not many of us have sufficient experience to back up our theoretical knowledge of the Bible. We know the truth and promises of Scripture doctrinally, but we lack adequate experiential learning to prove that the Scripture is true. There's no aspect of our spiritual formation and Christian experience where this deficiency is most easily identifiable and deeply felt other than prayer. Many believers will tell you that God answers prayers, yet many have come to embrace the myth of unanswered prayer. There are Christians who have explained away their weak and result-lacking prayer life by hiding under the notion of God's will. And it is as if the will of God is an abstract concept that cannot be known on this side of heaven. So, in this chapter, my focus is to examine and unmask the unanswered prayer myth because you can have what you ask for in prayer. You can shape your world through prayer if you let God's word shape your prayer culture.

In building a viable and effective prayer life, it's expedient that the myth of unanswered prayer is explored in the light of God's word as revealed through Scripture. The easy way to lead a weak prayer life is by embracing a concept that's not Scripture-based and allowing our experience to justify the Scripture. And as in any other aspect of our Christian life, the Scripture should explain our experience and not the other way around. The Scripture is the boundary of our knowledge of God's salvation. For this reason, we must tackle any foundational problem in prayer with fundamental principles found in Scripture. So, I'll be sharing two fundamental principles of prayer as revealed through the Scripture that we need to use in erecting the right foundational pillars for our prayer life. My desire is that you can review your prayer experience and be edified to build a more effective and productive prayer life. As Christians, whatever is allowed to attack and drown our prayer life can reduce Christianity to an ordinary and non-essential way of life on this side of heaven. The time is ripe for believers to become empowered witnesses of God's power to save, heal, deliver, and prosper in a world bedeviled by the forces of darkness, diseases, and poverty.

Before looking at these two principal principles of prayer, it is crucial to remind you of God's testimony of Himself and His ability to answer prayer. So, in God's dealings with Jeremiah, He declared the following words to him in Jeremiah 33:1-3:

"¹While Jeremiah was still confined in the courtyard of the guard, the word of the LORD came to him a second time: ²"This is what the LORD says, he who made the earth, the LORD who formed it and established it—the LORD is his name: ³"Call to me and I will answer you and tell you great and unsearchable things you do not know"" (NIV). The above Scripture must come to you as the revelation that God's delight is to answer you when you call upon His name. Just as the word of the Lord came to Jeremiah, God's word must come to you by faith today that the God we come to in prayer is the Great One who made the earth and established it. As such, as far as it relates to our journey under the sun, there's nothing that we need that God cannot supply. There's no place under the sun that we will go that God's hands cannot reach to deliver, save, heal, and prosper us. There's no bondage from which He cannot deliver us, neither is there a pit too deep that His hands cannot reach, nor a path too steep to walk on that God's hands cannot uphold us and keep us from falling. So, if you feel confined in life like Jeremiah was in the above text, know that you can call upon the Lord, and He will answer you. Our God is faithful, and His word is His bond.

David's testimony in Psalm 40:1-3 should be a faith inspiriting reading to your heart. He says, **"¹I waited patiently for the LORD; And He inclined to me, and heard my cry. ²He also brought me up out of a horrible pit, out of the miry clay, and set my feet upon a rock, and established my steps. ³He has put a new song in my mouth— Praise to our God; Many will see it and fear, and will trust in the LORD." (NKJV).** David's testimony shows that it doesn't matter what burden we bear today nor how long we've borne such a burden. We serve a God who rewards those who patiently wait for Him in prayer. God can bring us out of the miry clay, and not just that, He's able to set our feet upon the rock and put a new song on our lips. So, if, as a believer, you've been singing the myth of unanswered prayer, you need to be ready to start singing a new song. A song of God's power to save and of God's faithfulness as the Father, who answers prayer.

God still expects His people to call on Him and wants them to expect Him to show them great and mighty things that they do not know. Imagine what great and mighty things could mean for you in your own situation you've been praying about or the ones you quit praying about. With such expectations, God will be moved to give us visions about tomorrow and the assurance such visions will be fulfilled. Small-minded people won't go far with God in prayer because the One they seek wants to show great and mighty things that will confound the wisdom of the wise and will make weak the might of the strong. When we approach God with the assurance that His integrity is committed to performing what His word says concerning us, we open the way for God to invade our space with His blessings. So, as I share the following two prayer fundamental principles, I encourage you to open your heart. Let the word of God bring you deliverance from the myth called unanswered prayers.

The first of the two fundamentals of prayer is that praying with sin consciousness defeats believers boldness in prayer. Many believers have been taught that the prayer of a sinner is an abomination before God. Such approach to our relationship with God as believers takes away our confidence in approaching God as a Father who cares and who is eager to answer us when we call. Scriptures such as the following have been weaponized in structuring our minds to perpetuate sin consciousness:

"For the Lord watches over the righteous and listens to their prayers; but he opposes those who do evil." (1 Peter 3:12, GNT)

"The sacrifice of the wicked is an abomination to the Lord, but the prayer of the upright is His delight." (Proverbs 15:8, NKJV)

"The Lord is far from the wicked, but He hears the prayer of the righteous." (Proverbs 15:29, NKJV)

While the Scripture texts above are clear about God's position on the prayers of the wicked and evil doers, they do not give God's position on believers' status with Him. Thus, many believers still approach God in prayer as if they are sinners, believing that the reason their prayers were not answered is because of their sins. Such approach to God and such beggarly approach to prayer make the myth of unanswered prayer appear true. So, we develop inferiority complex and come to the Lord always believing that our sins will hinder us from experiencing the fullness of God's blessings because we have failed.

Yet, as believers in Christ, we have covenant rights before God in prayer and we must become conscious of who we are, our position in Christ, before God. Right from the Old Testament, the Scripture informs us that God is the covenant-keeping God to Israel. He says in Isaiah 43:25, **"I, even I, am He who blots out your transgressions for My own sake; and I will not remember your sins." (NKJV).** This Scripture is now fulfilled in Christ. Believers in Christ are no longer sinners even if they commit sin because God has changed their identification. Hear this:

[18]Now all things are of God, who has reconciled us to Himself through Jesus Christ, and has given us the

ministry of reconciliation, ¹⁹ that is, that God was in Christ reconciling the world to Himself, not imputing their trespasses to them, and has committed to us the word of reconciliation. ²¹For He made Him who knew no sin to be sin for us, that we might become the righteousness of God in Him." (2 Corinthians 5:18-19, 21, NKJV)

Friends, God is no longer imputing your sins against you because Christ was made sin for you. And in Christ, you have been made the righteousness of God. So, to think that your sin will hinder God from answering your prayers is to not believe God's positional view about who you have become to Him in Christ. The reason God told Israel He would blot out their transgressions and remember their sins no more is because of Himself and not because of Israel. If you want to go far with God, it's best to see yourself as He sees you. When you begin to walk in the realities of redemption, your prayer life will take on boldness, not in your abilities or self-righteousness, but in all that God has accomplished for you in Christ. Believers have become God's righteousness in Christ and God says, He no longer impute your sins against you, and He will remember them more.

How should you respond to this? Believers are to come before the throne of God with boldness. Come knowing that you are His righteousness through Christ. Come knowing that God's basis of acceptance of your prayer is not because of you but because of Christ. Hebrews 4:16

says, **"Let us therefore come boldly to the throne of grace, that we may obtain mercy and find grace to help in time of need" (NKJV).** Believers are to come boldly to the throne of grace knowing that they belong to the family of God. It is our gospel right; it is a legal right to enter into God's very throne. We must lose our sin consciousness and instead have Son consciousness. Hear this, **"For he has rescued us from the dominion of darkness and brought us into the kingdom of the Son he loves"** (Colossians 1:13, NKJV).

Friends, prayer will become a delight if you allow God's word to shape how you see yourself in Christ and live out your faith and pray. When we choose to give utmost attention to the word of God and embrace all that God has done for us in Christ, we have boldness to call God our Father. When we begin to take pleasure in what God's word has said about us, we will no longer be sin conscious, and sin will have no more dominion over our lives. Those who so live conscientiously before the Lord, knowing who they are in Christ will soon find out how much God is committed to hearing their cry.

Believers who constantly look into the word of God and allow the mirror of God's truth to shape them will have their outlook in life transformed by the power of prayer. They will prove through their experiences that God is the present help in times of trouble. Any believer who desires to travel far and deep with God in prayer must learn to come knowing that they are a part of Christ's body, who

Himself is the head of the Church, His body. And wherever the head goes, the body follows, boldly. Hear this: **"And God raised us up with Christ and seated us with him in the heavenly realms in Christ Jesus." (Ephesians 2:6, NIV)**. This is our reality and the reason for our boldness before the Lord in prayer.

The second prayer fundamental is that **praying outside the will of God is praying amiss, and it takes away the guarantee that God will answer our prayers.** The Scripture sheds light on this in James 4:1-3, saying, **"¹What is causing the quarrels and fights among you? Don't they come from the evil desires at war within you? ²You want what you don't have, so you scheme and kill to get it. You are jealous of what others have, but you can't get it, so you fight and wage war to take it away from them. Yet you don't have what you want because you don't ask God for it. ³And even when you ask, you don't get it because your motives are all wrong—you want only what will give you pleasure" (NLT)**. The above Scripture shows that while it is possible to have what we ask, God will not be moved to answer us if our motives are wrong. If everything we pray about is for our pleasure only, we have not met the prerequisite heart condition upon which God can release prayer answers. There are Christians today whose focus has been shifted off Christ, and the most profound motivation in their hearts in prayer is to want what others have. It's why Christ warns us in His prayer teaching in Matthew 6 that we must be careful so that our lives' motivation is not the same as that of the Gentiles (people who don't know God). Christ affirms that food, shelter, and clothing must not be our preoccupation with life and prayer. He then unveils what the right motivation in prayer should be. He says, **"But seek first the kingdom of God and His righteousness, and all these things shall be added to you" (Matthew 6:33, NKJV).**

As someone who has experienced what it means to have very little, I know how difficult it is to internalize and follow Christ's instructions in the text above. When you're unsure where your next meal will come from or how to pay your rent, it can be challenging to have the right motivation to seek God's kingdom. Yet, I also know by experience that if we can discipline ourselves and allow the Lord to help us seek His kingdom and His righteousness, He'll freely give us those things (food, shelter, and clothing) without adding any sorrow. He will provide us with health to enjoy our wealth, and we'll not have to spend our wealth on managing our health. So, if we desire to have power with God through prayer, the love of God must reflect in the content of our prayer. If all we've ever prayed about are things that will add to our pleasure because we covet what others have, God will not be obliged to answer us when we call. If this is the way we've been training ourselves in prayer, we will have little or no power in the days of real trouble. But if we have been seeking the kingdom of God and its righteousness through prayer, then we will experience the kingdom of

God whenever we call upon the Lord on the day of trouble and distress. Romans 14:17 says, **"For the kingdom of God is not eating and drinking, but righteousness and peace and joy in the Holy Spirit" (NKJV).** It means that if we have built a culture of seeking the kingdom of God in prayer when trouble comes and distress arrives, God will grant us the power and wisdom to make the right decisions in righteousness; He will fill our hearts with His peace, and His joy will be our strength! In our walk with the Lord, we cannot just arrive at a place where we are able, by the power of God, to be in command of any challenges that come our way. Our ability to manage the inevitable days of distress lies in our pursuit of the kingdom of God and His righteousness. Doing this will filter our motives and ensure we're aligned with God in words and deeds.

Now, the Scripture did not leave us blind on how we can seek the Kingdom of God in prayer. In our Lord's teaching on prayer, He included these words, **"Your kingdom come. Your will be done on earth as it is in heaven" (Matt. 6:10, NKJV).** The secret to building a powerful prayer life that we can draw from is hidden in seeking the will of God over any and every matter. The moment our motivation in prayer transcends materiality and pleasure is when our hearts begin to seek after the kingdom of God and the will of God. I am aware that some of our needs in life are intangible. However, this does not change the need to seek the kingdom of God and His will in our lives. For example, praying for the fruit of the womb, healing, and deliverance are intangible and essential. Still, they do not change God's will for us to procreate, be healed, and be delivered. So, most of what we call unanswered prayer is so because we do not know the will of God, and we have not prayed according to the will of God. In the day that we become preoccupied not by the gravity of our needs nor by the volume of our burdens, but by seeking God's kingdom and knowing His will over our cares, we will begin to experience the true power of prayer.

The guarantee for our requests in prayer comes from knowing and doing God's will for our lives and our needs. And the moment God's will becomes our preoccupation in prayer, we will begin to experience the supernatural power of God in real life and real-time. We see this assurance in 1 John 5:14-15, which says, **"¹⁴Now this is the confidence that we have in Him, that if we ask anything according to His will, He hears us. ¹⁵And if we know that He hears us, whatever we ask, we know that we have the petitions that we have asked of Him"** (NKJV). There must be no doubts in our hearts that the God we serve desires to answer and grant us our petitions; He's the same yesterday, today, and will be the same tomorrow. It means then that the most important prayer we can pray is that **Thy kingdom come. Thy will be done.** If we can so train ourselves in prayers, our spiritual senses will become activated to know the will of God for our lives and everything that concerns us. When our prayers are shaped and informed by the pursuit of God's will for our lives, finances, businesses, health, marriage, ministry, and children, we will begin to know the extraordinary power of prayer and the inexhaustible authority that's in the name of Jesus Christ. We will experience God's peace that transcends all understanding; We will overcome the powers of darkness and be freed from the shackles of anxiety.

The greatest prayer Christians should pray is **Thy kingdom come. Thy will be done.** When prayer, for you, becomes labor for knowing the will of God, then prayer becomes the means of executing God's good pleasure over your life and destiny. The way to pray and have what you ask is open, and perpetually so, only to the seekers of God's kingdom and His will. The way to have God's unhindered attention whenever you pray is to become someone God can partner with to do His will in your life and manifest His grace through your life's affairs. It is still God's desire to make Himself known; It is still God's good pleasure to demonstrate His treasure and power through our human vessels. However, this can only happen when to us, prayer becomes the pursuit of God, His will, and His righteousness. Therefore, when we come before God in prayer, we must come with open hearts to receive what's on His mind as touching our request(s).

So, I invite you to check your heart and your motives in prayer. When last did you intentionally pray about the kingdom of God? When last did you pray to know the will of God for your life, business, marriage, and parenting? When last did you pray about the will of God for the ministry God has committed into your hands? Is your prayer life about food, comfort, shelter, clothing, and other mundane things? Does it matter to you what God thinks about your life and its current direction? I encourage you not to gloss over the above questions. Your responses to these questions will show you how God sees your prayers considering His kingdom and will. God is looking for believers who are passionate about His kingdom on this side of heaven. If there's nothing about our lives that intersects with the interest of God in our homes, families, churches, and communities, it would be difficult for us to have power with God. God is looking for those He can trust with the treasures of heaven. And they must be people whose motivation to pray is not limited to eating, drinking, and self-gratification.

The prayer of many Christians today is overly marked by their desires for financial and material prosperity. Yet, those things are supposed to be the additions that attend our lives when we have yielded ourselves to the pursuit of God's kingdom and righteousness. There are believers today who are always in need of deliverance from satanic and demonic attacks and manipulations. The reason is that the activities of their lives are constant openings for the powers of darkness to invade their space. It is time to change that and enter your inheritance as heirs of God and co-heirs of God with Christ. I ask you again to check your heart to see how your pursuit and labor in life have fared in light of the kingdom of God. The reason you're saved is not so that God can bless you, heal you, or provide for your needs. You're saved so you can take your place in the Kingdom of God and be the extension of God's will on the face of the earth. So, ask yourself, how does what I'm asking God for imparts the kingdom of God? If there's no link between our prayers and the matters of the kingdom of God, it shows that God cannot trust us yet. As such, we cannot always have what we ask.

Take a look at 1 John 5:14-15 again from *The Passion Translation*: **"¹⁴Since we have this confidence, we can also have great boldness before him, for if we ask anything agreeable to his will, he will hear us. ¹⁵And if we know that he hears us in whatever we ask, we also know that we have obtained the requests we ask him."** Again, we can see that what moves God in our prayer is that our desires are agreeable with His will. Today many Christians speak about the permissive will of God as if that's a thing to be desired. By the permissive will of God, they believe that a decision must be God's will because it looks good, sounds right, and won't hurt anyone. No wonder many Christians have become people who have the form of godliness but deny the power of God. Until our lives are in sync with God, we'll have no confidence, let alone have great boldness in prayer. But when our will is lost in God's will, and we want nothing but God's good, perfect, and acceptable will, we enter a realm where we know that we'll obtain what we ask for whenever we call on God in prayer.

When this shift occurs in our lives, knowing God becomes a delight, and serving His purpose becomes our life goal.

I invite you to take a few moments to pray. You don't have to live one more day under the myth of unanswered prayer. The roadblocks that hinder others from pressing deeper into God do not have to stop you. Instead, you can become a part of a generation that seeks God, calls upon His name, and desires to see His kingdom come. There's a choice before you today. That choice is that you'll embrace the narrow path of intentionally seeking to know and do the will of God and let God have all of you. In the next chapter, I will expand on this, speaking about faith and prayer.

CHAPTER FIVE:

OF FAITH AND PRAYER

**"As for God, His way is perfect; The word of the Lord
is proven; He is a shield to all who trust in Him."
(Psalm 18:30, NKJV)**

Our understanding of the power of prayer will not
be complete without addressing the intersection
between faith and prayer. Amongst Christians today,
many well-meaning preachers and teachers of God's
word, regardless of religious titles, have hurt many hurting
believers. These preachers tell folks that their unanswered
prayers are due to their lack of faith. For example, someone
may be praying for physical healing, and instead of getting better in their health, nothing changes, or things
get worse. A preacher then explains that if only the sick
person has enough faith, they will receive their healing.
In another instance, someone praying and exercising
faith in a situation might be accused of buying into false
hope or giving the same to others for believing in God

for the impossible. Each of the above cases describes the overall experience amongst Christians today. I say this from my observations and experience with church life in the last two decades. Yet, we serve a great God who wants more than anything to show Himself strong in the world today through believers who call upon His name in Spirit and in truth.

So, in this chapter, I'll like to share how faith intersects with our prayer life. Experienced men like David continue to echo God's faithfulness throughout all generations. In Psalm 18:30, David declares, **"As for God, His way is perfect; The word of the Lord is proven; He is a shield to all who trust in Him" (NKJV)**. It's unarguable that God's way is perfect; it is a fruitless effort to think and seek to show that God's word is unproven. Many faithful saints have proven through their tenacious intentionality in pursuing God that His word is accurate, faithful, and reliable. In Psalm 12:6-7, David again declares: **"The words of the Lord are pure words, like silver tried in a furnace of the earth, purified seven times, You shall keep them, O LORD, You shall preserve them from this generation forever" (NKJV)**. Undoubtedly, God keeps His side of the bargain and watches over His word to bring it to pass. "He is a shield to all who trust in Him." God's word is no respecter of persons; He will keep His promises as true to all who trust in Him. He does not count on multitudes, but if the multitudes can put their trust in Him, He will fulfill His promises to them. Unfortunately, biblical and contemporary history has shown that this is not always the case. In every generation, only a few remnants of people seek after God. In contrast, others rely on human wisdom and canal strength to advance in life.

In your journey with God, take this challenge from me that you will choose to be numbered amongst the few measures their advancement in life by God and genuinely call upon the Lord because they trust Him and have Him as their only hope. For **"Some trust in chariots, and some in horses; But we trust in the name of the Lord our God" (Psalm 20:7, NIV).** So, we pray because we do not trust in the wisdom of our flesh to gain speed in the journey of life. Instead, we pray to arrive at the heights of fulfillment in God's time and without delay. We call upon His name because we do not trust in the strength of our bank accounts, human connections, professionalism, and family pedigree in winning the battles of life. **"For we are the circumcision, who worship by the Spirit of God and glory in Christ Jesus and put no confidence in the flesh" (Philippians 3:3, ESV).** Our sole trust is in the name of the Lord and in the power of the Holy Spirit. Our confidence in the Lord is why we ceaselessly call upon His name. This confidence drives our determination to live by faith, fail by faith, and prosper by faith. If this is clear in your mind, I want you to journey with me as we come before the Lord, praying that He will unfold to us what it means to have faith in God when we pray.

To unfold the secret of faith and prayer, our Lord Jesus gives us a parable on prayer in Luke 18:1-8. It says, **"¹Also [Jesus] told them a parable to the effect that they ought always to pray and not to turn coward (faint, lose heart, and give up). ²He said, in a certain city there was a judge there who neither reverenced and feared God nor respected or considered man. ³And there was a widow in that city who kept coming to him and saying, protect and defend and give me justice against my adversary. ⁴And for a time he would not; but later he said to himself, though I have neither reverence or fear for God nor respect or consideration for man, ⁵yet because this widow continues to bother me, I will defend and protect and avenge her, lest she give me intolerable annoyance and wear me out by her continual coming or at last she come and rail on me or assault me or strangle me. ⁶Then the Lord said, listen to what the unjust judge says! ⁷And will not [our just] God defend and protect and avenge His elect (His chosen ones), who cry to Him day and night? Will He defer them and delay help on their behalf? ⁸I tell you, He will defend and protect and avenge them speedily. However, when the Son of Man comes, will He find [persistence in] faith on the earth?"** (Amplified Bible Classic Version).

The parable above shows prayer is more than a mere tool for accomplishing a task. It reveals that prayer is the lifestyle of those who have come to place their absolute trust in God. This level of commitment to prayer happens only when we have reposed total confidence in God. It explains why we can choose to pray and do so until the results come. When challenges arrive and our adversary raises his fiercest battle against our lives and destiny, prayer is the only way to not chicken out and become cowards. Our Lord Jesus clarifies that it's either we're praying, or we're fainting and giving up. He paints the picture so vividly that the opposite of prayer is not prayerlessness but fainting. Prayerlessness from the parable above is not that we do not pray; we quit praying before the answer comes. This should be enough challenge to our faith; It should make us want to cry out to God for help.

In the parable, Christ portrays prayer using the symbols of a city, an unjust judge, an adversary, and a widow whose options are limited because she's poor. In the First-Century Roman world, widows had three obstacles to overcome in their pursuit of justice. First, they had no standing before the law. Second, they had no rights; third, only a man could lodge a complaint because women usually could not go before the court for justice. However, money and reputation could produce exceptions. The setback for the widow in the parable is that she's poor. With this in mind, we see Christ give us the picture of a widow who will not take a no for an answer. Christ shows that against all odds, the widow did not stop bothering the judge until her request was heard and justice was served. Imagine how many people would have attempted to discourage her; imagine the ridicule and the oppression the poor widow would have had to endure. She probably had all the genuine reasons to make her quit, faint, lose heart, and give up. But she refused to turn coward and pressed on until she had what she petitioned before the judge. The unjust judge said, **"Yet because this widow troubles me I will avenge her, lest by her continual coming she weary me" (NKJV)**.

Christ's parable establishes the first thing true faith in God does in our hearts. It is the propelling force that keeps us perpetually in the place of prayer until God hears our cries and answers us from His sanctuary. Like the widow, Christ expects His chosen people to have that energy to go against all odds and stand against all opposing discouragement in calling upon God. God wants us to pray day and night until He, the righteous judge, attends to our case. This idea must be firmly established in our hearts. As God's chosen people, we ought to pray and not lose heart. We are to pray, and pray, and keep praying until the answer comes; We are to pray always, constantly, and consistently; We are to pray without ceasing. There's a place in our Christian life that God wants us to reach; It is the place where we have emptied ourselves of our trust in money, power, influence, connections, and wisdom. It is a place where God becomes our all in all things and for all things. It is a place where we have come to the personal conclusion that without God, we can do nothing! Until we have reached this place, we may have no desire to pray. Our hearts will quit the place of prayer too quickly and prematurely. We will give up all too soon over the serious issues of life. This belief system separates the average believer from a true disciple of Jesus Christ.

Jesus asked a question at the end of that parable that should strike a chord in our hearts. He asked, **However, when the Son of Man comes, will He find [persistence in] faith on the earth?"** With this question, Christ shows that those who possess biblical faith have resolved that nothing in this world can separate them from trusting in God's ability to save, defend, and protect. If this is not how we understand faith, we have believed in error. And the time of liberation is now. Hear me, those that God promises to reward are those who will patiently persist in seeking after Him. It means that impatience is an enemy of faith; It implies that haste is not your friend when pursuing God's answers to life questions. Hebrews 11:6 says, **"But without faith it is impossible to please Him, for he who comes to God must believe that He is, and that He is a rewarder of those who diligently seek Him"** (NKJV).

The need for persistency in prayer shows that no one who seeks God impatiently will ever find Him; No one who seeks God for other things outside of God will ever find Him. Those who will experience the reward of finding God pursue Him, not for things, fame, or gold, but for Him. If our motive falls short of Him, our faith will fail in the place of prayer. Jesus clears all doubts about prayer, making sure we know that the matter of faith is not for the faint-hearted. Prayer is for those who know that even if they can't see God, He is, and even if they have no proof to show for their prayers, they know He hears them. The need for persistency in prayer requires that we will not trivialize the call to stay with God in prayer. It presupposes that many will be discouraged and bail out before help comes. We will have to pay closer attention to the text when it says, **"For he who comes to God must believe that He is, and that He is a rewarder of those who diligently seek Him."** This must take a deep seat in our hearts because if the just must live by faith, they will have to do so by embracing the pain of patience before enjoying the bliss of reward.

So, friends, we must take a cue from the widow in Christ's parable who chose to weary out the judge instead of losing heart. As a parent, I know what it means for my children to weary me out with their requests. And when they persistently press me for anything, it's either I take care of their concern, or I make a promise of when their concern would be addressed. The good news is that God is unlike human parents. So, in Luke 11:13, Jesus says, **"If you then, being evil, know how to give good gifts to your children, how much more will your heavenly Father give the Holy Spirit to those who ask Him"** (**NKJV**). The above text elucidates that we're incapable of wearying God out. He's a Father with inexhaustible provision for all of our needs. Our God is unlike the unjust judge in the parable above. He is our Law Giver, our King, our Righteous Judge, and above all, He is our Father. He will defend, protect, and ensure that the righteous are not forsaken. Praise God!

It's vital to say that Jesus' comparison between our earthly parents and our heavenly Father shows that the provisions for our needs are sealed in the Holy Spirit. All the answers to our prayers have been made available in the Holy Spirit. So, when Christ places the matter of prayer in the context of a court, it implies we need an advocate. We need someone who will competently represent us before the Father. That personality is Christ Himself. He is the Mediator of the New Covenant, our Great High Priest over the House of God. Consequently, so that we do not live our lives as orphans and in the pool of uncertainty, He sent us the Holy Spirit as our seal, and guarantee that will constantly have His witness within and with us. So Romans 8:26. It says, **"Likewise the Spirit helps us in our weakness. For we do not know what to pray for as we ought, but the Spirit himself intercedes for us with groanings too deep for words" (ESV).** This is what holds the key to understanding the true meaning of faith and releases the power to tarry in prayer until an answer comes. If we must stay persistent in prayer, it must be that the Holy Spirit is helping us. If we desire to receive the verdict of our just Judge and Father in prayer, we need the witness of the Holy Spirit within our hearts.

So, in our prayer cries to God, authentic and biblical faith means that we're walking and working with the Holy Spirit to receive God's judgment and justice over our case(s). For too long, many believers have thought that prayer is informing God about their pains. Others come before God thinking they could argue and convince God about the things that bother them. This explains why faith has become reduced to a powerless religious concept. I encourage you to let the word of God renew your mind today to know that faith is not wishful thinking nor endlessly waiting for something to happen. Faith in prayer is seeking a divine verdict over a matter, and it requires that we yield entirely to the Holy Spirit. Faith in prayer makes prayer a communion with God and not a one-way speech-making process. Faith is the foundation for a prayer relationship with God.

For this reason, effective prayer is laboring to know the will of God over every matter. When what we seek is not to have our own way but to know the verdict of God. The good news is that God has assured us that He will arise on our behalf to defend, deliver, and protect His own. When we become conscious that the context of prayer is the courtroom of heaven, we will come with humility and allow the Holy Spirit to communicate God's mind to us. We yield to God when we enter His gate with thanksgiving in our hearts and His court with praise. So, we can wake up daily declaring, "this is the day that the Lord has made." We know each day offers another opportunity to commune with God and hear afresh from Him about His will for the affairs of our lives.

The faith that Christ hopes to find at His return is the faith that is informed and sustainable by knowing and doing the will of God. It is a faith motivated by a deep, intimate, and intentional communion with God. The kind of faith that God will have regard and reward for is the one that desires to see the kingdom of God come and His will done over the powers of darkness. So, the question to ask is, "Is the will of God an abstract concept?" The answer is NO. God's will can be known, and God's will can be done. So, how can we know the will of God? We know the will of God by searching the Scripture and with the help of the Holy Spirit. What's interesting is that these two are inseparable. In John 6:33, Jesus says, **"It is the Spirit who gives life; the flesh profits nothing. The words that I speak to you are spirit and they are life"** (NKJV). It means anyone who desires to know the will of God in prayer must be a student in the school of the Holy Spirit and a committed student of the Bible. The will of God for our prayers is first and foremost contained within the pages of Scripture before they are revealed to us by the Holy Spirit. The Scripture offers us the promises of God and insights into His ways. Through the revealed word of God, unrelenting and unwavering confidence in God is born in our hearts.

In our battle against the kingdom of darkness in a dying world full of sin, sicknesses, diseases, and poverty, our victory in prayer is guaranteed only when we fight from the perspective of the word of God. This is the only way to fight from the position of victory and not for victory. If our spiritual exercise and warfare will be rewarding and meaningful, we must battle from God's incorruptible word. Our best example in this matter is Christ and His victory over Satan when the devil came to tempt Him in the wilderness during His earthly ministry (Matthew 4:1-10). Three times, the devil came at Christ to tempt Him in matters of the lust of the flesh, the lust of the eyes, and the pride of life; three times, Jesus conquered him by declaring IT IS WRITTEN. Therefore, the guarantee of unlocking prayer power is knowing what has been WRITTEN and invoking it over any matter that troubles and bothers us. To be clear, our first go-to for knowing what **IS WRITTEN** is our Bible. Anyone who hopes to accomplish great things in prayer must not be ignorant of sound biblical teachings on the subject they are praying about. In our Bible, we have the spoken words of God written for us so we can have words of authority to speak over our lives and our situations.

Knowing God's verdict over any matter starts by living a life of reading, meditating, studying, applying, and speaking the Scripture in our daily lives. As a disciple, the book that should be the most important to you is the Bible; the book you should read the most is the Bible; the book you should study the most is the Bible. When we begin to encounter the Life and Spirit sealed within the pages of the Scriptures, we begin to gain authority and experience the power of prayer. When we begin to allow the Scripture to guide our imaginations in prayer, we will begin to access the spiritual intelligence we need for our lives. God will start to communicate with our spirit by the witness of the Holy Spirit, and the mind of God will become revealed to us. This is where winning faith is born, and prayer becomes a prophetic declaration of the mind of God. We then begin to live, speak, and look victoriously upon our circumstances by this faith. When we have received the proceeding word of God for our lives, and we allow it to inform our spiritual exercise, the power of God will accompany our prayers. Our campaign against the forces of darkness that seek to steal, kill, and destroy our joy, health, finances, families, and communities will end victoriously.

I have found that if our prayer does not address the problem of poverty and lack, it's addressing the powers of sicknesses, diseases, the fear of death, or our need for fulfillment. So let me share two practical stories of how God-inspired words activated in our hearts can release answers to our persistent prayers. The first is a personal experience. The biggest challenge I have ever dealt with is the challenge of lack; I know what it means to lack and how to look up to God in prayer for His provision.

In 2008, I was a second-year seminarian, and accessing funds for my seminary education was a tall order. I must mention that at the time, I lived in Nigeria, where a federal student loan was unavailable, and scholarships were quite rare to come by. So, if you went to school, it most likely meant that your parents paid tuition for you, or you paid for yourself by doing side hustles. The challenge with such a reality is that I came from a humble background where raising funds for our education was a great sacrifice from our parents. Not only this, my conviction about stepping into the pastoral ministry and submitting myself for seminary education came with the instruction to do full-time education. It meant I could not do any side hustle to support myself. Instead, I had to depend on God and the support of my parents. So, at this time in school, the end of the semester was near, and the school made sure to inform us that without offsetting our bills, we wouldn't be allowed to write our final exams.

Now, I had been praying three months earlier from the start of the semester for God's provision for my tuition, but I did not receive any provision. I had been praying and reminding God of His promise in Psalm 23:1, which says, **"Because the Lord is my Shepherd, I have everything I need!"** (TLB). So, the burden in my heart was, "why would God send me to the seminary and would have no money to fund my education?" So, a particular morning came before the start of our finals. I went to our local church to pray and bear my burdens before the Lord. After I had prayed for some two hours, God spoke clearly to me from Psalm 27:13, saying, **"I remain confident of this; I will see the goodness of the Lord in the land of the living"** (NIV). The moment this word came to my heart, my burden was lifted as tears of joy flooded my eyes. My heart was moved to pick up a hymn book, and I sang the hymn titled **"It is Well with My Soul,"**[8] written by Horatio G. Spafford in 1873.

As I sang the hymn, I came to the fourth verse, and the first line became animated and stood out to me. It says, **"And, Lord, haste the day when my faith shall be sight."** Oh, what a joy that filled my heart as I sang that verse repeatedly that morning. At that moment, I knew that the provision I needed to offset my school bill was at hand, and that's precisely what happened. I finished my prayer and went home rejoicing, knowing that I would see the goodness of the Lord in the land of the living. And as such, it is well with my soul. When I got home, I met my dad with a smiley face as he shared the good news with me. A family friend came for a visit and had just left. Before leaving, he gifted my dad with some money twice the amount I needed to offset my school bill. If you've not experienced lack before, it would be difficult to appreciate the import of such supernatural provision. But this and similar experiences were God's ways of preparing me for the future and what has led me to where I am and what I am doing for the Lord today. I have learned that in everything God is leading me to do, I must obey Him by faith, and He continues to prove Himself faithful until this day. So today, I can say to you that Psalm 23 is not just a text of Scripture I know doctrinally, but I know it by experience. It is a living text that I live in. There can be no adventure or project that God will ask me to embark upon that can scare me financially. I know that so far, He's the Shepherd that I have submitted to; I have everything I need.

The second story I'll like to share relates to how standing upon God's word can bring about a medical miracle. As a local pastor, a couple got married in the church I served in October 2009. After a few months into their marriage, it became clear that it would take a miracle for this couple to have children of their own due to biological issues. The doctors had done their tests and judged that the husband had a low to zero sperm count. Now for Nigerian Africans, it's essential to know that in the culture of our people, childbearing is the glory of a wedding. It is expected that a just wedded couple should get into the business of childbearing immediately after their wedding. Where this does not happen, it is a call for concern that mounts undue pressure on the couple. So, a childless marriage falls short of the cultural norms for marital fulfillment. That's the context of our prayer for this couple. The couple prayed; As their pastor, I prayed, and I led the church to pray. One of the texts of Scripture that informed our prayer is Exodus 23:26. It says, **"There will be no miscarriage or infertility in your land, and I will give you long, full lives."** We began to pray, standing on this and similar promises in Scripture for this couple. Over time, God began to speak to this couple directly, assuring them that they would have their own children. But they had to wait until God brought changes to their biological situation.

As God would have it, on a particular morning in the early weeks of the last quarter of 2014, God spoke to me through a night vision. In the vision, I saw that the couple was blessed with their own child, and I was there at the naming ceremony where I gave names to their child. I knew immediately that this was the answer we had been waiting for. So, in the strength of that revelation, I called the couple and boldly told them that God had answered their prayers. All that was left to do now was to thank God and wait for the manifestation of His promises. Oh, won't He do it! God came through swiftly, and in the following month, the couple came to share the good news that the wife was now with a child. Their joy and my joy were doubled a few months later when the couple came to share with me that they were expecting a set of twins. And by the grace of God, in April of 2015, I was at the naming ceremony of those children, where I gave them names and rejoiced with the family as we celebrated the faithfulness of God. For this couple, God blessed them with two children of their own after five years of marriage and waiting upon God in prayer. Praise God!

I have shared these stories with you to stir your faith in God and let you know that God's word is still relevant for your particular situation today. When our faith in prayer is informed by the word of God and the inspiration of the Holy Spirit, there can be no telling of what God can do. When we allow the word of God to shape our lives and inspire our prayers, we open the door for greater possibilities if we can persist in prayer. When God answers our prayers, He first answers them spiritually before the answers will manifest physically. So, we need the Holy Spirit to help us receive God's response to our prayers. Sometimes, God's response will come by a strong impression in our hearts as we pray; at other times, it will come to us through our dreams, open visions, and other spiritual experiences. And still, at other times, God may send someone unaware of what we're going through to us to share a word that will address our particular situation. The Scripture remains the foundation of God's response(s) to our prayers in all of this. And He employs different channels of His choosing to communicate to us in a spiritual accent we will understand.

I don't know what challenges you've been going through that seem not to disappear. I don't know for how long you've been battling your challenges. I don't know how long you've prayed for something to shift in your life, so you can experience joy in abundance. However, I know that God hasn't changed; His power can still save, deliver, and prosper His chosen people who call upon Him in truth. So here are some questions for you "do you know what God is saying about your situation? What has God said to you about the pain you feel and the distress you're going through?" If you don't know what God is saying to you, pray until you do. And if you know what God has said to you, hang on to His promises and keep speaking them over your life and situation. Give voice to

God's word and allow Him to shape and refine your heart until His word sets your feet upon the rock. Sometimes, all God wants to do is change our prayer and realign our orientations according to His will. For example, while the couple I shared their story above received their own biological children, God could have told another couple to adopt a child(ren) and become parents to an orphan. What persistent prayer does is align us with God until our will matches His will. Whenever we allow this to happen, we can stand tall amid challenges, and what stopped the progress of others will have no power over our lives.

Look at Joseph in the Bible; he had two dreams about how great he would become in the future. However, he had to go through many trials, dangers, toils, and snares until God fulfilled His promises. Nevertheless, Joseph hung on to his dreams and refused to compromise his faith. In his many troubles, he remained unbent by the evil that surrounded him and never let go of God's word. Listen to what the Psalmist says about Joseph: **"He sent a man before them–Joseph–who was sold as a slave. They hurt his feet with fetters, He was laid in irons. Until the time that his word came to pass. The word of the Lord tested him. The king sent and released him, the ruler of the people let him go free. He made him lord of his house, and ruler of all his possessions, to bind his princes at his pleasure, and teach his elders wisdom"** (Psalm 105:17-22, NKJV).

I say to you, if you can pray until you receive a word from the Lord and allow that proceeding word to shape and govern your dispositions towards life, God will watch over His word to fulfill it. I am persuaded that If God reveals His verdict about your situation to you, He will perform it. If God shows you what He's about to do with your condition, He will bring it to pass. This is the heritage of all the saints of God. We are not victims but victors; We are not enslaved people but children. The Holy Spirit is waiting to help you and guide you into the truth about your life, marriage, children, and about your destiny. The Spirit of Christ is waiting to enhance your prayer, so you can pray and not faint. God wants to speak to you via His word. He wants to come into your dream and show you that all things are possible with Him.

God wants to give you an impression about your situation that will be real to you as the floor beneath your feet. So, I say pray in the morning and not lose heart; Pray in the evening and not turn coward; Pray ceaselessly and not faint. When you do, God Almighty will come to your defense; His right hand will work out salvation for you. His promises shall be established in your life. What ails you today? Where does it hurt today? What do you want God to do for you? Is it healing from physical ailment or deliverance from emotional and spiritual pains? Do you want to be freed from the bondage of lack and retrogression? Are you in limbo and need God to show you the way to go? Go to God in prayer and call upon His name. He will hear! He will show you great and mighty things!

CHAPTER SIX:

PRAYER PATTERNS

**"Great deliverance He gives to His king, and shows mercy
to His anointed, to David and his descendants forever."
(Psalm 18:50, NKJV)**

I n this chapter, I'll like to look at two biblical characters whose prayer life are patterns we can emulate. This
is necessary because God's on the lookout for men and
women with whom He can shape the next generation of
believers. Looking at all that we have shared on prayer, we
need to see how others have applied these principles and
got results. God wants to use our prayer life to advertise
His business in this generation and in the next generation.
So far in this book, we have learned a lot from the life of
David. And now, I'd like to use his words to introduce us
to the two characters I want to share with you. After his
song in Psalm 18, David declares, **"God gives great victories to his king; he shows constant love to the one he has
chosen, to David and his descendants forever"** (GNT).

The above text shows the reality that must mark our lives as we seek God in prayer. Through the power of prayer, we must bring into our lives and our world God's great victories so that the world can know that God's not dead, He is alive, and He is alive forever. God is looking for individuals that will demonstrate His power and wisdom to an unbelieving generation. God needs believers who will show that it's possible to constantly walk in righteousness and experience God's miraculous power and favor every day of our lives. God desires to use our prayer lifestyle as a legacy to teach younger generations about His works and ways. God wants to send a message to this generation and the next so that no one will have an excuse for rejecting the heralding of the kingdom of God.

Kathryn Twitty wrote the song **"Teach Me How to Pray,"**[9] which Jim Reeves sang. I found the song's lyrics to reflect the realities of many of our lives today. The lyrics say:

"One night, a sleepy little boy knelt beside my bed,

He smiled and looked into my eyes, and this is what he said,

Daddy, my daddy, you've taught me lots today.

So, daddy, my daddy, teach me how to pray.

You brought me home a brand new kite, showed me how to fly,

And there ain't no wonder kid whose dad can knock a ball so high.

I'd like to thank God for you, but I don't know
what to say.

So, daddy, my daddy, teach me how to pray.

I'd had to turn and leave his room; he began to cry.

I didn't want my boy to know, but so did I,

His best pal forsaken him, but what was there to say?

For daddy, yes, daddy had forgotten how to pray."

Like the daddy in Twitty's song, many dads, moms,
leaders, and even pastors today have forgotten how to
pray. And if you happen to be one of them, it is not too
late. It is not too late to turn a new leaf and learn the art
and act of prayer that you can bequeath to the next generations of people who look up to you. God wants His
people to pray. He wants to teach them how to pray, but
He'll like to begin with a few through whom the fire of
prayer revival can spread like wildfire. Throughout the
history of God's dealings with His people, He had always
given them patterns to follow in all their labor of building
things for God. When God wanted to build an Ark that
would save the people of the then world, He charged Noah
with the responsibility of building the Ark according to
a pattern. From the Ark's dimension to instructions on
selection and arranging the procession of animals into
the Ark, the Bible says, **"And Noah did according to all
that the Lord commanded him" (Genesis 7:5, NKJV).**
When God needed a Tabernacle in the days of Moses, He
commanded Moses to build everything according to the
pattern that was shown to him on the mountain (Exodus

25:9,30,40). When Solomon was going to build a temple for God, his father David gave him the pattern according to divine revelation (1 Chronicles 28:11-12, 19).

It is evident that God is meticulous every time He wants anything done, and in our own time, as He's building His Church, His methods have not changed. What God is building now is not physical temples. Instead, He's building individuals who will serve His purpose on the earth from the cradle to the grave. God is looking for people whose hearts are turned heavenward that He can use to turn the hearts of many heavenward. Therefore, God invests Himself in human temples to model what He seeks to accomplish in each generation. Hear this exhortation from the Apostle Paul in Philippians 3:17-19: **"[17]Brethren, join in following my example, and note those who so walk, as you have us for a pattern. [18]For many walk, of whom I have told you often, and now tell you even weeping, that they are the enemies of the cross of Christ: [19]whose end is destruction, whose god is their belly, and whose glory is in their shame–who set their mind on earthly things" (NKJV).** The text above shows that human patterns are God's favorite in building up believers who will become steadfast in their walk with God and in their services for God.

So far in this book, we have seen that people who pray are those who truly mind the things of the kingdom of God. They are people who desire to see the kingdom of come and His will done in their lives and communities.

To this end, I'll like to show you two men whose prayer lives had a significant impact on the lives of people around them. I hope that your heart is stirred into action through these characters. I hope you'll seek to become entirely determined to embrace a lifestyle of prayer that can show forth the glory of God.

The first individual to consider is Daniel, the man whose name means God is My Judge. The average believer today knows the story of Daniel and how the mouths of lions were shut for his sake. However, many are unaware and unfamiliar with the quality of Daniel's prayer life that produced such a supernatural feat in the land of Babylon. Many believers are like the children of Israel who only know the deeds of God, but His ways were hidden from them (Psalm 103:7). Supernatural things don't just happen; if that were so, it would mean that Daniel just got lucky. Supernormal and superhuman things don't just happen; if that were so, that would have been the norm amongst us today as God's people. Yet, we serve the God, described in the Bible as the Almighty. In men like Daniel, we see the embodiment of everything we have discussed on prayer in this book. Come with me with an open heart to glean wisdom for our own living from the life of this legend of faith.

The first thing Scripture reveals to us about Daniel is that he was a man who embraced the discipline of holiness and righteousness right from his youth. As one of the selected young men to be trained in the service of the Babylonian king, Daniel had access to the bounties and delicacies of the palace for three years. Yet, the Bible says, **"But Daniel purposed in his heart that he would not defile himself with the portion of the kings delicacies, nor with the wine which he drank; therefore he requested of the chief of the eunuchs that he might not defile himself"** (Daniel 1:8, NKJV). This text shows that Daniel didn't just become a man for whom God can deploy His angels so he will not become food for lions. Daniel was a man who had a clear understanding of what it means to be consecrated unto God. He knew what it means to be defiled and did all within his power to guide himself against every form of defilement in a pagan land. Daniel knew who he was, whose he was, and whence he came. He chose to be an Israelite even under captivity and lived by the laws of his God.

To have a prayer life upon which God can release His power, we must live in constant awareness that we're not of this world. Our way of life must show the consciousness within our hearts that we are of God and from Him. We, too, must build immunity around our lives against all the constant tactics of this world to bring defilement to our spirits and soil our garments. We have to be a people set apart in clear terms from the patterns of this world if we are to have the will to shape the world and shape the world around us. We cannot afford to live our lives like the rest of the world and hope to bring change into the world. Like Daniel, we must call defilement what others call delicacies, enjoyment, and entertainment. We must risk being the odd people in the room so we can be the ones to usher in the wisdom of God that will befuddle the wise men of Babylon. We must seek to dare the consequences of saying no to what the majority are saying yes to so we can stand out for God. If our prayer life will be worth anything, we must be a people who have found the narrow path that leads to life. Our feet must be removed from the broad way that leads to death and an empty way of life void of God's manifest power and presence. We must be a people who have the fortitude to confront the constant pressures of everyday life to dishonor, disobey, and disregard the laws of God for the pleasures of this world. Like Daniel, we must embrace consecration as the first secret to leading a victorious and prevailing prayer life.

The second thing about Daniel is that he was a man who knew God and knew how to get God to hear his requests with answers. Daniel's prayer life is highlighted throughout the pages of the book of Daniel. His consistent disposition toward prayer is the prime cause of his fortitude and wisdom all throughout his lifetime in Babylon. Here is how the Bible captures Daniel's prayer life: **"Now when Daniel knew that the writing was signed, he went home, and in his upper room, with his window open toward Jerusalem, he knelt down, and prayed and gave thanks before his God, as was his custom" (Daniel 6:10, NKJV).** One thing that's clear in this description of Daniel's prayer life is that anyone who seeks to have power with God must do so by building a prayer custom before the Lord. Daniel's life is reemphasizing that prayer must not be left to chance, nor must it be occasioned by challenges. Our drive for prayer must be traceable to a custom we have adopted. We must see prayer not as a tool but as a custom, a way of life. Like Daniel, the only way we can effectively confront the evil in our days is by building a power bank through prayer customs. When the powers that ran things in Daniel's day signed a policy that forbids the Jews to pray, his immovable prayer life became his means of protest.

Today, many Christians only pray when troubles come. We rush at prayers at the instant of hell's attack against our health and well-being, our families, careers and professions, and our flourishing ability. Little wonder our prayers are ineffective. But not so with Daniel. He had the prayer custom of bending the knee three times, which served as His reservoir of strength in the days of distress. As you may know, it takes a great deal of time to build a lasting custom. If you doubt this and, if you're a leader, try to change something that has become a custom or tradition with the group you lead. You'll be met with such a resistance that may likely make you doubt if the change you're attempting to bring is necessary in the first place. So, saying that prayer has become a custom to Daniel means it is a long-established practice over a certain period. Daniel could be less worried when arrested and thrown into the lions' den. At the end of the day, he told the king, **"My God sent His angels and shut the lions mouths, so that they have not hurt me, because I was found innocent before Him; and also, O king, I have done no wrong before you" (Daniel 6:22, NKJV).** What a testimony!

Daniel knew that if God hadn't condemned him to die by the mouths of lions, no lion, regardless of its fierceness, could lay a tooth upon him. Only those who have embraced a lifestyle built on Christ's righteousness and prayer can become uncompromising non-conformist believers amidst the godlessness of this generation. Our audacity to stand for God in life-threatening situations must be established upon the foundation of prayer customs. So, I ask you, what is your prayer custom? When will you develop your prayer custom if you don't have one? Let Daniel's prayer tradition speak to you today; Let his prayer life become both descriptive and prescriptive revelation. I ask that you let the Holy Spirit work upon your heart this season. You need to build a prayer custom that can shake off the powers of darkness and shut the mouths of lions that are constantly roaring against all that is good and godly in your life. When you have embraced a prayer custom, there will be no bad news that God will not give you the strength to handle. Only those who have built such relationships with God can have the effrontery to say what Daniel said to the king. They are the ones who know and who will know by experience that God is an ever-present help in times of need (Psalm 46:1). They are confident that God will command His angels to guard them in all their ways (Psalm 91:11).

One way to measure the quality and depth of our faith is by looking at our attitude in times of distress and trouble. Notice that Daniel could say, **"MY GOD sent His Angels…"** (emphasis mine). It means Daniel had a relationship with his God, and he knew enough that his God would show up to be the covering of his defenseless head in the days of battle. Notice also that he was described as a man who **"knelt down, and prayed and gave thanks before HIS God, as was his custom"** (emphasis mine). Like those who worship pagan gods testified to Daniel's devotion, people around us must know who we are and what we believe. You and I must ask ourselves, **"can we as individuals call God, My God?"** and can others describe us as individuals who **"pray and give thanks to his/her God?"** Until we build a lifestyle of constant personal conviction and communion with God, we cannot see the mighty power of God work the miraculous and the impossible amongst us. In a society bedeviled by the same spirit of Babylon that seeks to force people to worship other gods outside of the God who created the heavens and the earth, the sure way of navigating all the landmines of hell is by building a dependable prayer custom with God.

What more can we see in the life of Daniel? In Daniel 10:1-3, we're told that Daniel wasn't just a man who had built a prayer custom with God; he also knew how to fast and pray long. The text says: **"¹In the third year of**

Cyrus king of Persia a message was revealed to Daniel, whose name was Belteshazzar. The message was true, but the appointed time was long; and he understood the message, and had understanding of the vision. ²In those days, I Daniel, was mourning three full weeks. I ate no pleasant food, no meat or wine came into my mouth, nor did I anoint myself at all, till three whole weeks were fulfilled" (NKJV). Here, we see a man who knows how to approach God by fasting until God sends help. When you read the rest of the passage, you'll see that the secret to receiving life-changing secrets from God is staying long in prayer and adding fasting to our prayers. If we want God to reveal His will to us with the adequate wisdom and understanding we need to pursue it, we must be a people who will journey with God through fasting and prayer.

If we hope to go far with God and get tangible results for our prayer, praying long is not an option. It must become a custom. Now, I'll say you check with your doctor to know what'll work best for you on fasting. However, fasting speaks about self-denial in our determination to seek God. We fast because we want to discipline the flesh so our spirit can reach out to God in deeper communion. Notice that we're not told that Daniel fasted all the time. Still, we're told that his mourning and prayer were occasioned by his people's ongoing captivity (Daniel 9). So, when we have a situation that needs God's intervention, fasting and praying is one way of showing our humility and dependency on God. You may choose to skip breakfast during your fasting and praying days in such a situation. You may choose to live on fruits during this time; or decide to cut your breakfast and lunch as you seek the Lord. Whatever you do, you must bear in mind that our fasting and prayer do not move God; we're the ones who will be changed because we prayed and fasted to seek God's face for our lives. Let me add that fasting should be something we do regularly and not just whenever we have a difficult situation on our hands. You should at least have a monthly day of fasting if you cannot have a weekly day of fasting.

Daniel's life offers veritable lessons in praying persistently; he stayed in prayer and fasted for three whole weeks. Yet, it's essential to let the Holy Spirit inspire you to fast in prayerfully seeking after God. Remember that we cannot rush God into giving answers to our prayers. Hence the need for building a persistent prayer life. We know that God has the liberty to answer us whenever He chooses. Our job is to seek Him until we get His response to our request. Persistency in prayer is our way of showing patience with God over our needs. We're seeing in Daniel's life that he went the extra mile with God until God encountered him. We, too, can break the power of the enemy called "average" in our prayer life. When we choose to go the extra mile with God, He'll add something extraordinary to our lives. He'll bring us the knowledge we cannot learn from school and wisdom that we cannot find in books.

Before I move to the next prayer character, it is expedient to show that Daniel was a man who understood how to fight and win spiritual warfare. A careful and comparative reading of Daniel 10:1-2 and Daniel 10:10-13 give us a window into the depth of Daniel's devotion:

"¹In the third year of Cyrus king of Persia a message was revealed to Daniel, whose name was Belteshazzar. The message was true, but the appointed time was long; and he understood the message, and had understanding of the vision. ²In those days, I Daniel, was mourning three full weeks" (Daniel 10:1-2, NKJV).

¹⁰Suddenly, a hand touched me, which made me tremble on my knees and on the palms of my hands. ¹¹And he said to me, "O Daniel, a man greatly beloved, understand the words that I speak to you, and stand upright, for I have now been sent to you." While he was speaking this word to me, I stood trembling. ¹²Then he said to me, "Do not fear, Daniel, for from the first day that you set your heart to understand, and to humble yourself before your God, your words were heard; and I have come because of your words. ¹³But the prince of the kingdom of Persia withstood me twenty-one days; and behold, Michael, one of the chief princes, came to help

me, for I had been left alone there with the kings of Persia" (Daniel 10:1-13, NKJV).

The text above shows that there are territorial powers we will encounter and battle with in prayer if we must see results come from heaven. The Scripture above speaks of two entities referred to as Persia's king(s), one was physical, and the others were spiritual. On the one hand, the event described in Daniel 10 happened in the third year when Cyrus was king of Persia (10:1). But, on the other hand, we're told that during the same time, the Angel sent to bring answers to Daniel's prayer was withheld for three whole weeks by the prince and kings of Persia (10:13). And while all of this was going on, Daniel was in the place of fasting and prayer. This shows that the invisible realm is as real as the visible realm. So, imagine if Daniel had quit praying after the first day of not seeing results? He may never have received answers to his prayers if that had happened. This is one of the reasons we don't quit too early in our prayer adventures with God.

In a hasty generation that promotes sensualities that constantly flashes the riches of this world before our face, we must remain vigilant. We must not be deceived to conclude that all there is, is what our natural eyes can see. We must remind ourselves that **"For we do not wrestle against flesh and blood, but against principalities, against powers, against the rulers of the darkness of this age, and against spiritual hosts of wickedness in** the heavenly places" **(Ephesians 6:12, NKJV).** To think otherwise is to believe in error. So, we must remind ourselves of our spiritual weapons and be willing to fight the good fight of faith the right way.

2 Corinthians 10:4 says, **"The weapons we fight with are not the weapons of the world. On the contrary, they have divine power to demolish strongholds" (NIV).** As believers, God empowered us to give satan a run for his money. The spirit-filled example of Daniel challenges us to fight the good fight of faith through a lifestyle of prayer. Each of us must become a warrior who understands spiritual pathways. This is why prayer is a spiritual exercise. We must seek the help of the Holy Spirit in navigating our prayer conquests over the powers of darkness. We must embrace the humility of asking for God's wisdom. And by the insights God supplies, we will experience divine guidance, interventions, and power in the affairs of our lives, families, local churches, communities, and nations.

The life of Daniel challenges us to go the extra mile and never settle for average. Daniel became a governor in Babylon and God's prophetic voice to both the gentiles and the Jews of his time through his walk with God. He declared and exemplified the efficacy of God's presence and eternal power over all the gods of Babylon. If God can find men and women who will set themselves apart and build prayer customs, God can animate their ordinary lives. As a result, believers will arise that will walk daily in God's power, doing extraordinary things for the kingdom of God. If you have been struggling lately in life, I ask that you let the life of Daniel encourage you to press deeper into God. He stood his ground until he overcame all the plans of the evil one. Daniel found a place in God, where all weapons fashioned against him failed. Through his prayer custom, Daniel knew and obeyed his God, and by Him, he did great exploit. The good news is that God hasn't changed. He can accomplish more than what He did with Daniel through us if we can seek Him. God can incubate your life and make you the vessel through whom His salvation will be revealed to those around you. Daniel had a lifetime influence over Babylon and witnessed the reign of five kings in succession because he walked with God and understood spiritual warfare. He held his territory for God because he had a prayer custom that God could work with. If God can find such disposition to prayer in us, He will use us to bring His kingdom to our own territories.

The second prayer pattern I'll share with you is Elijah, the Tishbite. Ever since I have been reading the story of Elijah, the primary truth that keeps re-echoing in my heart is that he was a man of God's presence. Elijah was a man who knew what it means to cultivate God's presence and live perpetually thereof. When Elijah appeared on the scene in Scripture, it was at a time when Israel had abandoned God. He came at a period when the people with whose patriarchs God had cut covenant had become apostates and had taken other gods as their god. So, when

Elijah appeared, he did so as the bearer of God's light and divine discipline. In 1 Kings 17:1, Elijah brought a powerful declaration of God's rebuke to Israel's rebellious king. It says, **"And Elijah the Tishbite, of the inhabitants of Gilead, said to Ahab, As the Lord God of Israel lives, before whom I stand, there shall not be dew nor rain these years, except at my word" (NKJV).** With that declaration, there would be no rain nor dew in Israel for the next three and a half years. God had found a man that could compel His rebellious people to seek Him in repentance.

If you're a kingdom man or woman, you should know God wants to work through you to turn the hearts of the people around you towards Him. You know that your life's mission must intersect with God's mission of reconciling the world to Himself. As such, the way to fulfilling God's mission through our lives is by walking with Him through a lifestyle of prayer. The most significant advantage we have when we begin to press into God through prayer is that we will live as the people of His presence and the conduits of His power. We will know what it means to say, **"As the Lord lives before whom I stand."** Only people who know God's presence can bring His witness to others in a state of apostasy. When darkness seems to cover the land and wickedness and rebellion towards God are on the rise, what will stop the advancement of hell power are not programs and methods. Like Elijah, we need people who can demonstrate God's presence and power.

The New Testament gives us the insight we need into how Elijah was able to confront king Ahab, who led Israel astray. James 5:17-18 says, **"¹⁷Elijah was a man with a nature like ours, and he prayed earnestly that it would not rain; and it did not rain on the land for three years and six months. ¹⁸And he prayed again, and the heaven gave rain, and the earth produced fruit" (NKJV).** The secret to Elijah's access to God's presence is the power of prayer. We now know that the force behind Elijah's ability to make one statement of twenty-four words that impacted the nation for three years and six months is earnest prayer. Elijah had prayed fervently until he knew that God would not allow his words to fall to the ground. He had prayed until he had the assurance that God would honor the words of His mouth before he made his appearance before the king.

In many Christian circles today, there seems to be the draught of miracles; the manifestations of God's power seem to be in short supply. And the reason is that there are only a few people amongst us who have learned the way of prayer. So, we live at a time where unbelievers are unattracted to the Gospel of the kingdom of God. Listen, it doesn't matter your service level to God in the kingdom; you need God's presence to bring profit into the kingdom. God has designed that our lives will be the conduits of His power and authority in the world today, and we must arise without failing. The time has come for us to press into God with conviction and audacity as we confront a world groaning under Satan's reign.

After three years and six months had passed, Elijah showed up again. He discomfited 950 prophets who had submitted themselves to the worship of Baal and Asherah. He brought them to Mount Carmel, where he proved them wrong by burning the set sacrifice with fire from heaven. He got the whole of Israel to the base of the Mountain to answer one question. He said, **"How long will you falter between two opinions? If the Lord is God, follow Him; but if Baal, follow him"** (1Kings 18:21a, NKJV). When he finished asking that question, the Bible says, **"But the people answered him not a word"** (1Kings 18:21b, NKJV). However, after Elijah had called down fire from heaven, the story quickly changed. The Bible says, **"Now when all the people saw it, they fell on their faces; and they said, The Lord, He is God! The Lord, He is God!"** (1Kings 18:39, NKJV). Praise God!

Our Christian witness will stand the chance of impacting more people when the manifestation of God's power can be seen through our lives. The world is waiting for the Church to manifest God's great power again, and we must rise to this challenge. In John 4:48, Jesus asserts that **"Unless you people see signs and wonders, you will by no means believe" (NKJV)**. I think it's safe to say that many people in our communities today fall in this category of those who **"will by no means believe"** except they see signs and wonders. So, there must be men and women amongst us who can demonstrate God's supernatural abilities over the affairs of humanity. In the days of Elijah, all they needed to sort out was what the truth was between the two opinions. However, these days, many philosophical thoughts are competing with the Gospel. Many arguments contend with Christ's claim as the way, the truth, and the life. Our chances of succeeding at sharing the Gospel are cut in half if all we rely upon is our good works, expertise, rational abilities, and eloquence power. We might be able to win some that way. However, they're many more that will be beyond our reach until we introduce the supernatural essence of God into the landscape.

To encourage our hearts and our resolve to embrace the lifestyle of prayer, let's take a look at James 5:17a from four versions of Scripture.

"Elijah was a man with a nature like ours (with the same physical, mental, and spiritual limitations and shortcomings) …" (Amp).

"Elijah was a human being just like us…" (NCV)

"Elijah was as completely human as we are…" (TLB)

"Elijah was a man with human frailties, just like all of us…" (TPT)

I hope this clarifies that we don't have any genuine excuse to not call upon the Lord until revival breaks forth in the land. We don't have to be angels; We can still be humans and have the supernatural treasure of heaven within our vessels. If we, too, can learn the way of prayer, we can bring the light of God into the dark places in our lives, families, local churches, communities, and nations. We can beat back the forces of darkness that seek to hijack all that is good and godly in our generation. If you can rise today and begin to call upon the name of the Lord like never before, it means the reign of darkness is numbered around your life and home. The grip of hell over your family, business, career, local church, and community will be put on leave notice. Stop telling yourself that you can't; Stop glorifying the limitations that make you human as the reason not to call upon the name of the Lord. If Elijah could do it, so can you; If Daniel could do it, so can we. And we shall in our lifetime do great exploits for God not my our might and wisdom but through the power of prayer! AMEN!

CHAPTER SEVEN:

THE WHOLE
PURPOSE OF PRAYER

"And I will pour on the house of David and on the inhabitants of Jerusalem the Spirit of grace and supplication; then they will look on Me whom they pierced. Yes, they will mourn for Him as one mourns for his only son, and grieve for Him as one grieves for a firstborn." (Zechariah 12:10, NKJV)

After looking at understanding the power of prayer thus far and several principles of God's word that can shape our lives and the lives of those around us. There is an emphasis that we cannot afford to leave out. This is necessary for our daily life, daily walk, and daily work for God as we move on in our Christian pilgrimage. This chapter will share what I consider the ultimate goal for building a robust prayer walk with God. The sole purpose of building a power-filled and power-dispensing prayer life is **to facilitate our speed and ability to live**

in the world as Christ is in words and deeds. Any prayer custom we try to develop without this goal in mind cannot accomplish much for the kingdom of God. God Almighty speaking through the prophet Zechariah declares that **"And I will pour on the house of David and on the inhabitants of Jerusalem the Spirit of grace and supplications; then they will look on Me whom they pierced. Yes, they will mourn for Him as one mourns for his only son, and grieve for Him as one grieves for a firstborn" (Zechariah 12:10, NKJV).**

The above text reveals that the chief purpose that occasions the outpouring of the Spirit of grace and supplication is so that we can look upon the pierced One. Our journey has not even begun in our prayer pilgrimage until we look upon Jesus Christ, God's only Son (Romans 8:32-35) and the firstborn among the dead (Colossians 1:8). It is Christ who was crucified, died, buried and brought back to life from the grave by the power of the Spirit to redeem us back to God again. The prophet Isaiah spoke about Christ in Isaiah 53:5. **"And He is pierced for our transgression, bruised for our iniquities, the discipline of our peace (is) on Him, and by His scourging we are healed" (Isaiah 53:5, LSV).** So, if we miss the point of looking upon Christ as the goal of prayer, we would have missed the whole counsel of God for our lives. If all our interest in prayer stops at receiving things from Him, our prayer would be indistinguishable from the prayers made by adherents of other religious beliefs.

When Zechariah prophesied, the coming of the Spirit of grace and supplication, it is to ignite a passion within God's people through prayer to look upon the pierced One. This is because there's a veil that can be removed only through prayer so we can genuinely behold Christ and be transformed. The apostle Paul declares, **"And we all, with unveiled face, continually seeing as in a mirror the glory of the Lord, are progressively being transformed into His image from (one degree of) glory to (even more) glory, which comes from the Lord, (who is) the Spirit" (2 Corinthians 3:18, Amp.).** It must be clear in our mind that we engage God in prayer to become transformed into the image of Christ. The Holy Spirit is outpoured upon us to reveal Christ to us and in us. Therefore, our understanding of prayer must be narrowed on Christ so He can broaden our scope of life in Him and for Him. God would answer what we ask in prayer so that our lives can reflect the glory in Christ Jesus and the realities of our inheritance in Him. If we miss this, we would have wasted our prayers on mundane things that perish and our spiritual investment on pleasures that fade away.

To make this crystal clear to us, the Apostle John tells us that **"Love has been perfected among us in this; that we may have boldness in the day of judgment; because as He is, so are we in this world" (1John 4:17, NKJV).** The ultimate goal of our communion with God is to find out about His perfect love for us and lay hold of it. It is to seek out the truth that His love for us is His love for the world and to help those in our world come into the same experience of the Father's perfect love as we have. To be in the world today as Christ is means we understand the reconciliation we have in God through Him and the ministry of reconciling others with God committed into our hands. If we fail to understand this, embrace it, and live by it, we would have defeated the whole essence of prayer.

Our daily living, speaking, walking, and working are designed, upon the experience of salvation, to reflect Christ's life in the world today. For this reason, we pray, and it is for this reason we need to look upon Jesus' prayer life. He's the ultimate pattern that should shape our prayer life. If we hope to accomplish anything worthwhile for God through our prayers, Christ must be our ultimate and singular focus. We may follow the examples of others only if they point us to Christ. However, the One we must hope to imitate is Christ. So, if God were to give us the same privilege He afforded Solomon to ask whatever we desire, our choice must be Christ. So, we must have the audacity to say to Him, **"Lord, I Want You."** The reason the love of God has come to us is so we can be like Christ in words and deeds. We need to look upon Christ's prayer life to know how we can function in the realities of His grace and power in the world today.

To understand Jesus' prayer practice, we will need to briefly explore His life in the Gospels. The Gospel evangelists show us a vivid picture of Christ as a man who prays. I'm not talking about Christ's prayers for others.

I speak about the depth of His prayer communion with God. Mark 1:35 says, **"Now in the morning, having risen a long while before daylight, He went out and departed to a solitary place; and there He prayed" (NKJV).** Here we are told that our Lord Jesus Christ was a man who knew how to rise early to pray. You will notice that Christ's prayer life was not a show of activity to impress anyone. His prayer life was a private adventure with God. So, long before others awake, Christ would take a journey and find a solitary place to have communion with God. Since He is our Lord, wc will do well to follow His example. We must learn to cut off every form of distraction from our lives and say no to prayer show-offs to truly have communion with God. Now is the time to accept Christ's privacy policy about prayer. The motivation for our prayer life must not be left in the atmosphere of public worship but behind closed doors where God can truly work upon our lives.

Further, Jesus' prayer practice is not just that He prays in solitary places; we are told that prayer was a lifestyle to Christ. In Luke 5:16, the Bible says, **"But Jesus Himself constantly withdrew into the Desert and there prayed" (WNT).** Other Bible versions use the words "often (The Living Bible)," "frequently (NET Bible)," and "as often as possible (The Message)" to describe Jesus' prayer culture. He knew how to withdraw from the busyness of ministry to a place where He could be alone with God. So, in Christ, we have a model that we, too, can pattern our lives after. We often think that life in the 21st Century is too busy for us to pray. We feel that we are too occupied with the demands of daily life, which leaves no time left to pray. It is time we allow Christ's life to renew our minds and set us on a path where we can develop a different prayer attitude. We need to build the habit of constantly withdrawing into our closet from all the busyness of life to have genuine communion with our Lord. We must allow Christ to be our Lord, even in this matter; We must allow all our best excuses to give way for the example of Christ to shape our lives. Matthew 14:23 says, **"And when He had sent the multitudes away, He went up on the mountain by Himself to pray. Now, when the evening came, He was alone there" (NKJV).** That is the example of the Christ!

Hear me. None of us can claim to be as productively engaged with life as Christ. The service He was rendering to the people was pulling crowds from Jerusalem and beyond. Yet, He had learned the necessity of stepping away from such a tight, engaging, and demanding schedule to slip into solitary places to have communion with God. In Christ, we must learn the secret of meaningful and productive living. That secret is not in keeping a busy schedule but in keeping the depth of our communion with God. In the text above, we're told that **"Now when evening came, He was alone there."** It means Jesus didn't practice a shallow, scurried, and hurried prayer life. He knew how to stay alone for a long time in God's presence. So, we have Christ as the example of how to accomplish great things for God in our different areas and levels of endeavors. A believer who is passionate about the kingdom of God should at least have an hour of daily alone time with God in prayer. We will make many mistakes in life and take many wrong turns in our Christian pilgrimage if we are not receiving daily wisdom from God in prayer. The measure of life in Christ is not how busy we are for God but how busy we are with Him.

One major blessing that we see in Christ's prayer practice is that prayer will give us the advantage of accessing deep, practical, and superior discerning abilities. In Luke 4:42-43, the Bible says, **"Now when it was day, He departed and went into a deserted place. And the crowd sought Him and came to Him, and tried to keep Him from leaving them; but He said to them, I must preach the kingdom of God to the other cities also, because for this purpose I have been sent" (NKJV).** Prayer offers us the best way to receive, retain, and run with God's visions for our lives with an accurate understanding and reach the place(s) of our fulfillment in record time. We will have many distractions (even productive labor can quickly become a distraction) and encounter many tempting attractions. The only way to stay sharp and alert for God is by building a habit of spending quality alone time with God.

In my experience, I know how difficult it is to follow our sense of divine purpose and journey in the direction to the place where that purpose will be fulfilled. Seven years ago, I made what I see as the most challenging life decision. At the time, I was the pastoral leader of a local Baptist Church in Lagos, Nigeria. Before I assumed the pastorate of this church, I planned to spend a minimum of 10 years in the church if God's people so desired. My decision was based on mini research I did about a few thriving Nigerian Baptist local churches. My findings have shown that such churches had the same pastoral leadership for at least a period of 10 years. So, I simply planned to spend 10 years minimum in each local church God would give me the privilege to lead.

Well, a year and a half into my sixth year of pastoral leadership in the church, both as a student pastor and the full-time pastor, God said I should get ready to resign at the end of my sixth year. So, I knew my time would be up, but I didn't know what the next step or place of assignment would be. As time progressed, nine months before my resignation, the answer came through prayer. I knew God would be sending me to the United States as a missionary according to His promises to me some 12 years prior.

However, when I submitted my resignation letter to the church three months before leaving, the church refused to accept the letter. I remember being called to a special committee set up by the church to convince me to stay. While I felt needed and appreciated such an opportunity to serve God, I knew my options were few. Either I obey God and satisfy divine pleasure, or I take the people's plea and dissatisfy God. Now, you would think I would have figured out how to get to the United States before my resignation, but I didn't. When it comes to doing the will of God, we do it by heart, not by our head. When I submitted my resignation letter, I had no money, no sponsor, and no visa for my transition to the United States. As if that wasn't difficult enough, God had led me to a seminary in the United States where tuition and living expenses were $45,000 per annum for a three-year program of study.

To be in my shoes meant knowing no one, dead or alive, that could sponsor me with such an amount of money for education. It also meant having no relations, no single person, in the United States. Yet, in this situation, like Christ knew in His heart, I knew I must preach the Gospel of the kingdom of God to peoples beyond the shores of Nigeria. So, I followed my heart, stayed with God, and moved in the direction of His calling for my life. Looking back seven years later, I know what it means for the just to live by faith. God has proven Himself beyond all reasonable doubts, for He will not send us to a place where His hands cannot provide for our needs.

I don't know in what capacity you are serving the Lord. Still, I can tell you that it is only through prayer that you can be at the right place, at the right time, doing the right thing in your service for God's kingdom. Only through prayer can you accurately discern what God calls you to do and where He calls you to do it. Some folks reading this might not be called into the pastoral ministry like I am, but that will not change your need for discernment.

You need discernment to prosper doing whatever you're currently doing for the Lord (including what you may call secular work). You need God's insight to know where to invest your money. If you are a parent, you need God's wisdom to raise your children and guide them in the direction of God's purpose for their destiny. If you are an employee, your chances of fulfillment in the organization you're working for will be limited without accessing God's will for your life. Ultimately, you need discernment to know how to contribute your quota in advancing God's kingdom, either in the marketplace or in the ministry.

I remember how almost all the older and senior pastors I knew counseled me against the foolishness of resignation. Yet I was resolved to follow God's lead I had known for a year and six months. Some thought it was youthful exuberance and ambition. Others were certain I would regret leaving the pastorate of a 'privileged church' and a life of certainty for an uncertain future. The only significant encouragement I received for making my decision was from my wife, two pastor friends, my parents (including my in-laws), and my siblings. My pastors were unsure how to counsel me, but they prayed for me. At the time, any other person I knew was stuck between encouraging what they perceived as ambition and discouraging me from making a costly mistake. Raising $45,000 per annum for school for a three-year study abroad from a very humble background is like hitting your head on a rock and looking for water in the desert. Yet, because it was not an ambition but the will of God, God made supernatural provisions available that continue to sponsor my journey until this day.

Furthermore, God connected me with my first sponsors, the late Deacon Gamaliel Onosode (of blessed memory), and his wonderful daughters. It would take more than a chapter to narrate the story of how I received sponsorship of $45,000 from Deacon Onosode for the first year of my education abroad. The fact that he gave the financial support without even knowing nor seeing me is something only God can do. Not only that, his daughters, who barely knew me, were moved by Deacon's generosity to pay for my flight ticket to Atlanta, Georgia. They did so before I got my visa, and they later supported me with enough money to leave with my wife and children before I traveled. For these individuals and many more, I am eternally grateful. I have seen God honor my obedience in countless ways than I could ever have imagined in the last seven years.

Hear this: The late Deacon Gamaliel Onosode, was a man renowned for his integrity and blessed by God. He understood the purpose of wealth and served God in financing many kingdom projects. And I have the singular honor to call him a sponsor, and the only recipient of such level of financial support made to an individual. I say all this to tell you that God still provides for His work, and He yet have many more selfless individuals like Pa Onosode, who have chosen to live such a life of legendary magnanimity towards God's people. However, it is when we neglect the will of God and fail to seek the kingdom of God and His righteousness that we struggle to make meaningful connections with our destiny helpers. Destiny helpers are not in short supply. It is our pursuit of selfish ambitions that darkens our discernment and make living and serving God a woeful and frustrating experience for many.

So, I ask that you consider your ways and get serious with God. As your Shepherd, the Lord's passion is to direct you to where the pasture is greener and where you will find rest for your soul. But if you cannot submit yourself to the direction He's sending you, you will become the victim of the limitations of your five human senses. If we are not going to miss out on the program of God for our lives, we must pray. We need superior discernment that's available only through the power of prayer to live above limitations. If we are not going to settle for all things lesser than the best of God for our lives, we must, through prayer, learn how to make decisions. If we do not want to end our journey in an inglorious position amongst the crowd, we must rely on the Holy Spirit. Our judgments in life must not be based on the compassionate plea of the public. Our life choices must not be informed by the well-meaning ignorant counsel of the few. We must learn to live and die by the proceeding word of God. We must rely entirely on what God is saying in our hearts by the Spirit of prayer. Don't get me wrong, there is a place for godly counsel, and I got mine from my spouse, pastors, friends, and parents. But in the end, I still had to discern God's voice for myself. And God helps you if your counselors are unable to hear from God and you take their words as counsels from the mouth of God.

Imagine what could have happened to Jesus' destiny if He had allowed that crowd to stop Him from leaving. Imagine what could have happened to the salvation of humanity if Jesus had allowed Peter's stern rebuke when Christ began to tell His disciples about His crucifixion (Matthew 16). There's a realm of glory that we cannot attain until we can accurately discern how God is moving in our lives. The best of God for our professional life, career, businesses, and ministries is hidden in the Holy Spirit. It is through ceaseless prayer that we can search it out. Our God is never late or too early, and blessed are they who know how to walk in God's time and walk into His plans. If you can discern your future by the Spirit of God, your perception of yourself will change. You will know that you are not a fatherless child. You will see that you are not a sheep without a Shepherd. You will learn that you're not as poor as society wants you to believe. You will know that your defense is sure, and your future is secured, colorful, and bright. There are riches in Christ for you that inflation cannot corrupt. There's a promotion in life for you that no one can deny you. There's a wealth of health and flourishing for your spirit, soul, and body that no virus can corrupt. Yet, without a constant prayer life, we may go about life without accessing all of God's provision for our lives. God's plan for us hasn't changed; Even today, the Scripture is still true: **"If they obey and serve him, they shall spend their days in prosperity, and their years in pleasures" (Job, 36:11, NKJV).** From the example of our Lord Jesus Christ, we know we can be in the right place at the right time. We know that accurate discernment will be available for us when we submit ourselves to a lifestyle of prayer. God wants to empower us to minister to and be a blessing to as many people as possible.

Christ's prayer practice shows that He did not only pray early in the morning or during the day; He knew how to pray all night. Luke 6:12 says, **"Now it came to pass in those days that He went out to the mountain to pray, and continued all night in prayer to God" (NKJV).** As part of our prayer culture, we must add the discipline of praying all night as much as we can. This type of spiritual discipline is necessary, so we can subject our flesh to the promptings and leadings of the Holy Spirit. Luke 6:13 gives us insight into why Christ chose to pray all night on this occasion. The Bible says, **"And when it was day, He called His disciples to Himself; and from them He chose twelve whom He also named apostles" (NKJV).** When you look at the above text, you will see a principle that should govern your decision-making processes.

For Jesus to appoint His apostles, He preceded His decision by praying all night. Notice that these apostles were the men upon whom the future of His life's work would rest. These were going to be the men responsible for propagating the gospel to the ends of the world. So, you would agree that aside from laying down His life for the world, Christ's decision here would go down as the second most crucial decision He made in His earthly ministry. Now, the Bible says Christ prayed all night to make such a decision. While many disciples followed Jesus at the time, His selection of those who would champion His course was never going to be informed by human sight but through divine insight. If Christ had to go through the discipline of all-night prayer in making such a life-changing decision, how can we expect to get things right without constant prayer?

Today, many Christians have been making bad decisions over time. The accumulation of those decisions has sent their lives in the wrong direction. The world's gravitational pull has limited so many believers from reaching their place of fulfillment and living their lives to the fullest. So many lives are stagnant right now, not because God has changed but because they did not consult Him before embarking on the journey that stagnated their lives. Excluding divine intelligence from our dealings allows satanic powers to prey on us. Whether in marriage or ministry, business or career, relationships or finances, we cannot go far apart from Christ. There are believers today who have made bad career choices, and their lives are full of regrets. Today, there are people whose ambitions in life have set them on a voyage where it would be difficult for them to fulfill their God-given purposes. So, before you make that destiny-altering decision, would you please consult with God? Before you make that trip and relocate your family, would you embrace the discipline of praying long enough until God's mind is opened to you?

The prayer life of Christ is an eternal model that shows us how to be prepared for life's unexpected troubles. Having a betrayal amongst His disciples after He had prayed indicates there are unavoidable challenges we'll encounter in life. This means that even decisions we make in obedience to God's will may not make our journey trouble-free. However, our ability to cope and press on, run and not be tired, walk and not be wearied when challenges come, rests upon whose voice we have obeyed. If you allow the Lord to be your guide, you will fear no evil, even though you walk through the valley of the shadow of death. The reason is that Scripture assures us of the presence of God when we allow God to be our Shepherd (Psalm 23). But if you run along in the pastures of your own imaginations, your security is not guaranteed. So, let me ask you, who ordered your current life's direction? Have you checked with God on that decision you are about to make?

Psalm 127:1-2 says, **"Unless the Lord builds the house, they labor in vain who build it; Unless the Lord guards the city, the watchman stays awake in vain. It is vain for you to rise up early, to sit up late, to eat the bread of sorrows" (NKJV).** It means there is no reason for us to labor in vain, and neither is there a reason for us to watch in vain. It indicates that anyone who knows how to submit to God's building prowess and timing through prayer will not be a victim of wasted years and effort. If life seems restless, it's time to pause and seek God. If nothing seems to be working out for you despite your qualifications and connections, it's time to pray. What you are missing is not the need for more struggle and hustling but the blessing of God that gives rest without adding any sorrow to it. The God we serve is not a taskmaster, and our heavenly Father is not one who does not care for the well-being of His children. Let the words you read come to you as an encouragement that's asking you not to go on in your Christian pilgrimage without knowing how to make decisions by the Spirit of God.

In the next chapter, we will look at two critical issues that constitute the content of Jesus' prayer. But as I bring this chapter to a close, permit me to say that it is possible to make the right decisions and secure the future in the present. Through the power of prayer, you can see the dangers ahead of you and avoid stepping into traps that will derail your progress and advancement in life. In Christ's prayer life, we know that it is possible to do the impossible feat of hitting all the right chords of time, being in the right place, at the right time, and doing the right thing at the right time. When we pray, we give God the allowance to sharpen our perception so that we can fly on eagles' wings and accomplish our God-given destiny through superior discernment.

Chapter Eight:

WHAT DID JESUS PRAY ABOUT?

**"Now it came to pass, as He was praying in a certain
place, when He ceased, that one of His disciples
said to Him, "Lord, teach us to pray,
as John also taught his disciples.""
(Luke 11:1, NKJV)**

If you were one of Jesus' disciples, you might be as
questioning as the disciple in the text above. You may
start asking questions like, what could He probably be
praying about that took Him so long? Why is His prayer
so effective? In this chapter, I would like to explore the
content of Jesus' prayer life with you. While it would be
rewarding to study the rest of Luke 11 to see what Jesus
taught His disciples about prayer, my primary burden is to
share what He prayed about for Himself. My hope is that
we, too, can take our journey with the Father as we glean
wisdom from the depth of Christ's communion with Him.
An idiom says, **"Don't give me fish but teach me how to**

fish." I don't know about you, but the best lessons of life that have shaped my life are those I learned by observing others doing the things I hope to do. The conviction I want to leave with you is that we can have access to the same fountain that produced the abundance of grace we see in Christ Jesus. If we know what Jesus prayed about, we can experience His abundant life in our lifetime. We can enjoy the same divine support He had if we follow His example. We can dispel the powers of darkness everywhere we go when we commit to a lifestyle of prayer. So, let's dive into what Jesus prayed about so we can begin to know what to pray about.

We do not know the content of Christ's first prayer in Scripture, but we know what that first prayer produced. Luke 3:21-22 says, **"²¹When all the people were baptized, it came to pass that Jesus also was baptized; and while He prayed, the heaven was opened. ²²And the Holy Spirit descended in bodily form like a dove upon Him, and a voice came from heaven which said, "You are My beloved Son; in You I am well pleased""" (NKJV).** There we have it; Jesus' first prayer produced the baptism of the Holy Spirit and brought access to the voice of God. In all the synoptic gospels–Matthew, Mark, and Luke, it's only in Luke that we are told that Jesus prayed at His baptism. What is the significance of this for us today? The answer is simple: if we hope to have access to the same power that worked in Christ, we will need to pray for the Holy Spirit's baptism (if we are yet to be baptized in the Holy Spirit) and be quickened to hear the voice of God. Today, many believers have experienced water baptism either by sprinkling or immersion, as infants or adults. Yet not many know what it means to be baptized with the Holy Spirit. So, if we desire to have a vibrant Christian life, then Jesus is showing us what to pray for. We cannot truly enjoy our inheritance in God until we know what it means to be filled with the Holy Spirit and what it means to hear the voice of God.

From Jesus' experience, we know that the evidence of His baptism in the Holy Spirit is that the voice of God was immediately heard when the Holy Spirit rested upon Him. This is the challenge that many people have; many believers do not know how to hear God when He speaks to them. And one significant consequence of not hearing God is that it makes divine guidance an uphill battle. This is why we pray; This is why we must pray. Our prayer should not be a preoccupation with the needs and wants of our lives but should be laboring to experience the presence and power of God. As we begin to know the presence of God, the voice of God becomes easy to discern. Prayer is the access we need to experience the presence of God's Spirit and for our spiritual senses to be activated so we can hear God. Until we know how to hear God's voice consistently, our journey on this side of heaven will be burdened with too many limitations.

Someone might be asking a question in their heart, saying, how does God speak today? The answer to that question is all over the pages of Scripture. First, as believers, we know that the Bible is the custodian of the voice of God. In Psalm 119:9, 105, the Bible says, **"How can a young person stay on the path of purity? By living according to your word" "Your word is a lamp for my feet, a light on my path" (NKJV).** So, anyone who wants to know the voice of God will do well to become friends with their Bible. By reading the written Scripture, we can stand the chance of encountering the living word of God. Hearing God's voice would be difficult for lazy Christians, and their experience with prayer will be limited.

2 Timothy 3:16-17 says, **"All Scripture is given by inspiration of God, and is profitable for doctrine, for reproof, for correction, for instruction in righteousness, that the man of God may be complete, thoroughly equipped for every good work" (NKJV).** I hope it's clear that ALL SCRIPTURE is inspired by God; from Genesis to Revelation, ALL OF IT. Every serious believer knows that they cannot claim to be Christians and be Bible illiterates simultaneously. God wants to lead, guide, guard, and prosper you, but we will hugely miss out if we fail to be good students of the Bible. Not on this, we must read, meditate, study the Bible through the life and the works of Christ. All of Scripture points to Christ (Luke 24:27, 44-45) and if our desire is to understand the Scripture and accurately apply Scripture in our lives, we must know that the Scripture is Christocentric. The facts that something appears in the Bible does not make it Christlike. Our

understanding of the Bible is not so much about looking for something that is 'biblical,' but all that is Christlike (Hebrews 1:1-3). If we miss this one, then every other way God speaks may not help us much. Every other means by which God speaks are only accessible through the Holy Spirit. And according to Christ, the Holy Spirit has been given to reveal Christ to us (John 16:13).

Further, Jesus said, **"It is the Spirit who gives life; the flesh profits nothing. The words that I speak to you are spirit, and they are life" (John 6:63, NKJV).** If we cannot pray, it would be nearly impossible to encounter the spirit and the life in the Scripture. If we cannot read the Scripture, it would still be challenging to experience God's spoken voice in the Scripture. Therefore, a believer must live a balanced prayer life and study the Scripture. Today's challenge is that many of us neither pray nor have time to read the Scripture. We live in a sensory world where we access the physical world through our five senses. Likewise, God wants to activate our spiritual senses to access the spirit realm. But without the Holy Spirit, we can never detect the things of God. He wants our spiritual eyes, ears, and hearts activated so we can pick divine impressions, signs, and symbols. But none of that would help us much without the infilling of the Holy Spirit. God wants to enliven the Scripture within your heart; He wants to give you dreams like He gave to Joseph (Genesis 37). He wants to provide you with visions like He gave to Ezekiel (Ezekiel 1) and show you signs like He did with Moses

(Exodus 3). God wants to bring you symbolic revelation like He did to Peter while he lodged in the house of Simon, the tanner (Acts10:9-16). These are spiritual realities that God wants to bring us into as navigating tools for our Christian pilgrimage here on earth. But many Christians may never come into this experience. And this will not be because God is unwilling but because these believers chose a life of spiritual laziness and prayerlessness.

The pattern we see in Jesus' prayer life is that it is possible to be filled with Holy Spirit. He showed us how we can hear the voice of God and exemplified that it is possible to know whether or not our lives are pleasing unto God. Here is where our prayer must begin. Today, we don't have to be victimized by the hurtful things others have said to us. And we don't have to be limited by the powers of darkness. When you see believers living under the condemnation of others, it is not because any human voice is stronger than the voice of God. The challenge is that we have failed to build a prayer life that can open the door to us to a place where the voice of God becomes natural to our hearts. But that must change! You must choose to come all out of the oppression that a human's voice has put you. If someone had said you will not amount to anything in life, you could break that spell upon you if you can pray. The believer who can pray is a powerful person. The believer who can be filled with the Holy Spirit can know no limits. The believer who can hear the voice of God will, against all odds, prosper in the land of the living.

If you grew up in a local church that gives no emphasis on the ministry of the Holy Spirit in a believer's life, I have a word for you. Ask God to help you shift your gaze upon Jesus. He alone must be our final authority for faith and practice. If He needed to pray until the Holy Spirit came upon Him and the voice of God came from heaven, so must we. Many believers today want to die before they experience heaven, which is fine. The problem is that they will not be of much use to God on this side of heaven. God is looking for believers who can bring heaven down to earth through the Spirit of the living God. We must not think it was a joke when Christ taught His disciples to pray that **"Your kingdom come. Your will be done on earth as it is in heaven" (Luke 11:2b, NKJV).** Listen, Jesus asked us to say such a prayer because He knew that God would answer our prayer. We can experience God's kingdom here on earth as it is in heaven. We can know, do, and fulfill God's will here on earth as it is in heaven. It is time to wake up! Any believer who is unfilled with the Holy Spirit cannot enjoy the riches of our glorious inheritance because those things are sealed, and the Holy Spirit is the guarantor (Ephesians 1:14). Any believer who cannot constantly be filled with the Holy Spirit cannot hope to be effective in the service of the kingdom of God. The Bible says, **"For the kingdom of God is not in word but in power" (1 Corinthians 4:20, NLT).**

For believers, life in the Holy Spirit is not an alternative; it is required. Our lives are empty without the Holy

Spirit, and we feel powerless without His help. Living without knowing the Holy Spirit exposes us to the manipulations and darts that come from the powers of darkness and the wickedness of men. Spiritually matured men like Paul warned us by saying, **"Don't be drunk with wine, because that will ruin your life. Instead, be filled with the Holy Spirit"** (Ephesians 5:18, NLT).

In Luke 24:49, Jesus told His disciples, **"And remember that I am about to send out my Father's promised gift to rest upon you. But, as for you, wait patiently in the city until you are clothed with power from on high"** (WNT). To be filled with the Holy Spirit is not an option. If it was not an option to those who first received the Gospel, how can we ever think it would be an option for us? As believers, we must come to a point where we say to God, "As for me, I will wait patiently upon You until you clothe me with power from on high." Let me remind you that Jesus did not begin His earthly ministry until the Holy Spirit came upon Him. The disciples never bore witness to Christ's death and resurrection until the Holy Spirit came upon them at Pentecost. Of a fact, Christ's disciples were already disciples before they became baptized in the Holy Spirit, and they never stopped being filled by the Holy Spirit. To think that we have another pattern for Christian living and service outside of being baptized and constantly filled with the Holy Spirit is to have been brainwashed by strange doctrines. It means the forces of hell will be mighty in our day when we fail to wait upon God for the enduement of power by the Holy Spirit. It implies that we won't accomplish much for God and His kingdom without the clothing and the equipping of power. Worst still, it means we can become victims of Satan's revenge against God and His people. If we fail to learn how to wait upon God consistently in prayer, we cannot win fighting the good fight of faith. Except we repent and go back to our own upper room where God forges His people with power, Christianity will not be so meaningful. No wonder Jesus never taught His disciples how to preach or teach, but only how to pray. If Satan can stop us from praying, he can strip us of power and do with our lives as he pleases.

I hope you can resolve in your heart that you will not go on in your Christian pilgrimage without the power that comes from the Holy Spirit. You don't need to be a pastor, prophet, evangelist, apostle, or teacher before asking God to fill you with His Holy Spirit today, tomorrow, and every day of your life. Peter assured the spectating crowd of this on the Day of Pentecost. He said, **"38Repent, and let everyone of you be baptized in the name of Jesus Christ for the remission of sins' and you shall receive the gift of the Holy Spirit. 39For the promise is to you and to your children, and to all who are afar off, as many as the Lord our God will call" (Acts 2:38-39, NKJV).** It's time to stop being a spectator of the move of the Holy Spirit in the world today. You, too, can join in on what God is doing these last days and experience the different capacities of grace available in the Holy Spirit. And the way to that experience is the way of prayer. The way to mix the patience to wait for the Holy Spirit with the courage to move into the world when the Holy Spirit prompts us is open to us through prayer. We must become people who pray before attempting to reach out into the world and witness God's saving grace through Christ.

After His baptism and overcoming temptation, Christ's ministry began in the power of the Holy Spirit. We only read that He constantly separated Himself to pray from then on. We do not know what He prayed about until His time of crucifixion drew near. He prayed for many, healed many, delivered many, and even taught His disciples to pray. Still, until the time of His suffering for humanity, we know not what He communed with God about. So, in Luke 22:41-42, the Bible says, "**⁴¹And He was withdrawn from them about a stone's throw, and He knelt down and prayed, ⁴²saying, "Father, if it is Your will, take this cup away from Me; nevertheless not My will, but Yours be done" (NKJV).** I have written extensively on the will of God in prayer in Chapter Four, where I emphasized that you can have what you pray for if you can pray according to the will of God. However, the perspective that Christ is giving us through His prayer here is that the will of God will not always be easy. It is important to note that in the prayer above, Jesus was not essentially praying to know the will of God. His prayer is that the will of God be done over and above the limitations of His flesh. It means there will be a time that the will of God will not be juicy and rosy but difficult, tasking, and full of challenges.

It means God may come for us and move us out of our comfort zone and demand that we let go of our ambitions and the pleasures we long to enjoy for the sake of His kingdom. Christ's prayer life teaches us that prayer brings us to a position in our spirit, soul, and body where we can truly and fully obey God. The example of Jesus shows that if we can genuinely ask the Lord to help us do His will, He will send us help. After Jesus had prayed in Luke 22:41-42, in verses 43-44, the Bible says, **"Then an angel appeared to Him from heaven, strengthening Him. And being in agony, He prayed more earnestly. Then His sweat became like great drops of blood falling down to the ground" (NKJV).** In this place of prayer, Jesus overcame the sufferings that were to follow. Here is where He experienced victory over the future in the present as an example that we, too, can possess the future in the present if we can pray. We can experience the help of God and the strength to obey Him if we can pray. God can send us spiritual and human angels to strengthen our Christian pilgrimage. Our ability to please God and carry and follow His will for our lives is made possible through prayer. So instead of constantly living under the burden of struggles, we can pray. We can stay in the place of prayer until our help comes from the Lord, the Maker of heaven and earth.

From experience, I know that sometimes when God wants to take us to the next levels, He commands our obedience in leaving our comfort zones. If He wants to help us, He'll bring one or two people to tell us the exact instructions He's been impressing on our minds. At other times, to help us, He'll make sure that He repeats that instruction so that we will be without excuses. I say all that to encourage your heart that if there's any area of your life where you are struggling to obey God, quit struggling and cry to Him for help. It would surprise you how willing God is to enable you to align with Him completely. When we ask for His help, we'll find out that the Scripture is true. **"For it is God who works in you to will and to act in order to fulfill his good purpose" (Philippians 2:13, NIV).** In our journey with God, we must learn that there's no alternative lifestyle for a life of obedience by emulating Christ. We must learn how to be as sincere as possible in asking the Lord to help us give Him our complete obedience.

I once heard the story of a recently licensed pilot flying his private plane on a cloudy day. He was not very experienced in instrument landing. So, when the control tower was to bring him in, he began to get panicky. Then a stern voice came over the radio, **"You just obey instructions, and we'll take care of the obstructions."** Our journey in life is like flying an airplane, and sometimes, doing the will of God can get cloudy and bumpy. So, instead of panicking and relying on our limited wisdom and strength, we can cry unto God for His help. Doing this shows that we recognize our feebleness before God, and for that, we can expect Him to send us His help so that our flight can enjoy a safe landing. There's a path to enjoying the flight of life that God has designed for our fulfillment and refreshing. This is the path to effective and powerful prayer life and is captured in Jesus' life testimony. He, like us, was tempted in every way but prevailed.

Hebrews 5:7-9 says, **"⁷In the days of his flesh, Jesus offered up prayers and supplications, with loud cries and tears, to the one who was able to save him from death, and he was heard because of his reverent submission. ⁸Although he was a Son, he learned obedience through what he suffered; ⁹and having been made perfect, he became the source of eternal salvation for all who obey him" (NRSV).** When Jesus walked this world, the Bible says, He prayed and cried with a loud voice. Yet, the reason God heard Him wasn't because He prayed but because of His reverent obedience and submission to the will of God. As great as Jesus was, what made God hear Him each time He prayed was not because He was the Son of God but because He learned obedience. If God so dealt with His Son, we should not expect Him to cut us some slack. God's ears are not deaf to our cries, and His hands are not too short to save and deliver us. However, our relationship with God can only be enlightened and deepened through our submission and obedience to Him.

In our Christian pilgrimage, learning to follow God's will and being filled with the Holy Spirit give two outcomes to our prayers. At Bethany, where He raised Lazarus from the dead, Jesus revealed what the outcomes of our prayers should be. After asking them to remove the stone that blocked the dead man's grave, John 11:41-42 says, **"Then they took away the stone from the place where the dead man was lying. And Jesus lifted up His eyes and said, Father, I thank You that You have heard Me. And I know that You always hear Me, but because of the people who are standing by, I said this, that they may believe that You sent Me" (NKJV).** In the above text, we see that the outcome of Jesus' prayer is that **"God has heard, and God will always hear."** And if we still believe that **"As He is, so are we in this world" (1 John 4:17b)**, these same outcomes must be evident in our prayer life. This is why prayer is not a one-time thing or a once-in-a-while thing. Prayer must remain a lifestyle and a journey to live like Jesus in the world today. As we live more and more like Christ, our prayer life will produce outcomes that will be in the order of Christ. This is the goal of prayer, to live like Christ in all things, even in our communication with God. This must be the focal point of our communion with God and the only labor to make our lives count.

I am resolved that Christ is the person I want to imitate; my life's goal is to know Him and make Him known. I want to be like Christ in words, deeds, and prayer; I do not believe there's a higher calling. The invisible Jesus is still in the world today by His Holy Spirit, looking for authentic believers to animate so He can continue His ministry of reconciliation. Christ still wants to demonstrate His great power over all the powers of the enemy and forces of darkness today through His church. We will do well to align ourselves with Him. I have seen God answer prayer in my life, and He continues to do so today. I still expect to see more extraordinary things in answer to prayer. God is calling you today to join forces with Him through prayer. There's no other way to living a changed life and no alternative to making a lasting impact in the world for God outside of prayer. If you can pray, you can shape your world. And if we can pray, we can shape the world for Christ.

CONCLUSION

T he call to prayer is one that every child of God must answer. The fact that you are a child of God means that you can pray, and it means that through you, God can do great things. It means that God has a witness on earth through whom His kingdom in heaven can find expression. That we are alive today as believers mean that the knowledge of the glory of God and His power to save can cover the earth as the waters cover the sea. If you are reading this and, in the ministry, it means God wants you to model prayer for the people you lead. Whether your ministry is on the pulpit or in the marketplace does not matter; what matters is that you arise in obedience. God wants you to join the generation of those who call upon the name of God. If you are a parent, it means you have work to do. God wants your children to be trained in the way of prayer and become His representative in their own generation. One of the privileges I have enjoyed in life for which I am eternally grateful is having parents who know how to pray, especially my mother. She laid such a foundation of prayer in my life that my existence is proof that God still answers prayer today.

I have a mother who sought the face of God in prayer before I was born and made specific requests from God about her fourth child. She prayed and told God she wanted her next child to be a dark-skinned son that would be blessed with sound health. My mother's prayer was occasioned by her experience as a mother. Before his first birthday, her first child died due to sickness, and she had two sickly surviving little children (male and female) before I was born. So, she prayed to God for a healthy male child that would know no infant nor childhood sickness and would have dark-toned skin. I can boldly say that I am the product of my mother's prayer, literally. While the rest of my siblings all have light-toned skins, including my parents themselves, I alone have dark-toned skin. In addition, unlike the rest of my siblings, I never experienced infant or childhood sickness the way they did. My mother would later have another son after me, and today, my parents, three siblings, and I are all alive and healthy. To God be the glory!

A lifestyle of prayer is the only way to accomplish what we cannot do with our natural strength. And in this world, there will be many things we cannot do by ourselves. We will be faced with life's circumstances in which the only way of escape will be to experience God's help from above. In our Christian pilgrimage, it would be impossible to please God nor serve Him productively without a lifestyle of prayer. For these reasons and many more, I encourage you to go and become doers of the word of God. Each chapter of this book includes prayer points; pray over them repeatedly until you come into the experience of your prayer. You are a viable instrument in God's hand, and God desires that your life will count in His plans. You will do well to arise with a great resolve to seek God through your commitment to prayers. Because of you, the kingdom of God will be known and experienced in your family, community, and the local church. God is willing to pour His Spirit upon you if you can call out to Him.

Perhaps you've read through this book because of sheer interest, but you are yet to receive the salvation that Jesus offers. If that describes you, it is my honor to introduce you to Jesus Christ. Through His death, burial, and resurrection, He has provided free forgiveness of sin and the gift of eternal life. You don't have to do anything or pay any money to receive His gift of salvation. Just say to Him, **"Lord Jesus, today I believe in the sacrifice You paid for my sins, that You died and on the third day, You rose again to give me eternal life. So, I receive your free gift of eternal life and I now have forgiveness through the riches of Your grace. I ask that You fill me with Your Holy Spirit and give me the confidence of the saints of God in Christ."** If you say that prayer, you're welcome into the kingdom of God. I encourage you to find a local Church near you where your faith will be nurtured, and you, too, can take your place in the kingdom of God and begin to serve God and His people.

I want to leave you with this assurance in your travels with God, my Christian brothers, and sisters. James 5:16 says, **"Confess your sins to each other and pray for each other so that you may be healed. The earnest prayer of a righteous person has great power and produces wonderful results" (NLT).** This should stir your heart to pray and never give up. There's a power that can come into a situation if you can pray. In God, you already have Christ as your righteousness, so don't let sin consciousness ruin your prayer life. If you can arise and pray, your prayer will produce incredible results. You don't have to get stuck in any situation; Our God is the God of great deliverance. You don't have to settle for the less, the will of God is the best that can happen to you. I know by experience that there's nothing I need that God won't provide. And the reason I know so is that my life has been forever poured out to do His will. So, whenever I call for provisions, He will answer me, and even before I call, He will supply my needs. I don't have to worry about my health; my mother's prayer ensured that I would enjoy sound health before my birth. Today, I am still withdrawing from her prayer bank for my life.

I want to ask you, "what will your prayer life produce for God?" You're a poor person if you've never needed God. A situation like that should send you crying earnestly to God for deliverance. It means you don't know what it means to live by faith. No one who obeys the call of faith will ever come to a point where they can do everything themselves. The only possibility where we can do all things is through Christ that strengthens us, and we get that strength only as we call upon His name in prayer. So, I ask you again, what will your prayer life produce for the kingdom of God? How many great things have you seen your prayer accomplish for God, and how many do you still want to see? When God says, **"Call to Me, and I will answer you, and show you great and mighty things, which you do not know" (Jeremiah 33:3, NKJV),** He has more for us. There's more in God and from God for us. There's more to Christianity than where we currently stand in God.

I say to you, go and pray! Build a prayer life that will become the platform for God to release and reveal great and mighty things. So far, you still number amongst the living; make your life count for God and for His kingdom. Go and pray and live as nearly as you pray. Go and become a man, a woman, a boy, a girl of God's presence and experience His power. I say pray until His kingdom comes. Pray until His will is done in the earth as it is in heaven!

Maranatha!

APPENDIX

Chapter One: Why Pray?

Let us pray: Heavenly Father, I come to You today because I know that You alone are praiseworthy. I ask that You deliver me from the ignorance that comes with prayerlessness and empower me with strength to call upon your name. By Your Holy Spirit, please enlighten my heart to comprehend the power of prayer so that I can serve You all my days in Jesus' name, AMEN!

Chapter Two: Prayer, A Spiritual Exercise

Let us pray:

1 Heavenly Father, I come to You today and ask that you strengthen my feeble knees.
2 Heavenly Father, I come to You today and ask that You do what You must in my life and make me a strong soldier of Jesus for the glory of your name.

3　Heavenly Father, I ask today that You begin Your work in my prayer life and make me to number amongst those who are constantly standing in prayer for my marriage, spouse, children, families, church, and community for Your will to be done.

4　Heavenly Father, please fill my heart with an insatiable hunger for You and an unquenchable taste for spiritual things. Please help me to seek after You and to know You as I am known.

5　Heavenly Father, I release my spirit, soul, and body to Your Spirit today. Please pour upon my life the Spirit of Grace and Supplication. Holy Spirit, I ask that from today forward, that You pray through me and manifest Your power over the kingdom of darkness through my life.

6　Heavenly Father, beginning from today, as I pray through the help of the Holy Spirit, let the power in the name of Jesus Christ find maximum expression through my life.

7　Heavenly Father, I ask that You make my feet firm like those of the deer, train my hands to war for You, and arm my arms with the strength that comes from Your Holy Spirit in Jesus' name, AMEN!

Chapter Three: Of Prayer Length

Let us pray:

1. Heavenly Father, I come this moment to confess that You are all I have. I ask that You be my strength, my shield, my helper, and my deliverer.
2. Heavenly Father, I ask that You deepen my root in You until my faith in You becomes unmovable. Please give me the grace never to lose heart until I too will see Your goodness in the land of the living.
3. Heavenly Father, through Your Holy Spirit, please lift the weights of weariness off me and cloth me with the strength of those who wait upon You.
4. Heavenly Father, by Your Holy Spirit, quicken my spiritual senses so I can hear when You speak to me and to accurately perceive the things You want to show me.
5. Heavenly Father, please grant me the grace to never again make haste over any concern in life. Teach me how to repose absolute confidence in You in prayer so I can walk in faith and by faith for the rest of my life.
6. Heavenly Father, I confess that I will not be one amongst those who turn back from You. Please work upon my heart, give me stability, and give me the wisdom to walk through life knowing that I have You as my King, my Father, and my All and All.

7. Heavenly Father, I thank You as You fill my heart with Your peace and receive my praise now and forever more, AMEN!

Chapter Four: You Can Have What You Ask For

Let us pray:

1. Heavenly Father, I come to You today and I ask that You bring Your search light over my heart. Search me, O Lord, and remove every defiling desires from my heart.
2. Heavenly Father, I ask that You fill my heart with the desire for Your will and the manifestation of Your kingdom in my life and through my life.
3. Heavenly Father, do Your works in me so I can number amongst the generation of those who seek You, not for gold nor glory, food nor raiment, shelter nor pleasure, but that Thy kingdom may come, and Thy will be done.
4. Heavenly Father, I come to You today and I ask that through Your Holy Spirit, let Your love be spread abroad my heart. Please grant me the grace to make You my first love so I can truly run the race You've set before me.
5. Heavenly Father, I ask that You give me the will to exercise my dominion in Christ over the power of sin. Fill me with might that I may come before You always with boldness.

6. Heavenly Father, I ask that You make me an instrument of Your peace so that through my life and my work, others may know Your love and experience Your grace.

7. Heavenly Father, I ask that You fill my heart with an undying compassion for Your kingdom, so I can live for You and not for myself. By Your Holy Spirit, please teach me how to pray and pray through until Your will is done in and through my life as it is in heaven in Jesus' name, AMEN!

Chapter Five: Of Prayer and Faith

Let us pray:

1. Heavenly Father, I come to you today to confess that I have nowhere else to go except to You. Please help me to never turn coward nor lose heart in the place of prayer.

2. Heavenly Father, I ask that You invade my thoughts with Your thoughts and be Thou my vision. Help me to think as You think and to see my situation as You see it.

3. Heavenly Father, I want to receive Your proceeding word about my life; by Your Holy Spirit, please give me a word for this season of life, a word to run with and a word to live by.

4. Heavenly Father, I ask that You open the eyes of my heart so I can see like You see. Let Your kingdom come, O LORD, and let Your will be done in my life.

5. Heavenly Father, by Your Spirit within me, give me the right insight and understanding I need to wait upon You and to experience Your power over my life, marriage, children, and business.

6. Heavenly Father, by Your Holy Spirit, please help me to overcome hastiness and learn how to wait patiently upon You until You move the mountains that I cannot move.

7. Heavenly Father, I release myself for the works of Your kingdom and the fulfillment of Your will. Please let my life serve Your purpose and permit no power of darkness, sin, sickness, diseases, or poverty to prevail in my life in Jesus' name, AMEN!

Chapter Six: Patterns of Prayer

Let us pray:

1. Heavenly Father, I come today and ask that you break down every limitation that keeps me from calling upon Your name.

2. Heavenly Father, I ask that You cut me off from every form of defilement so I can call upon Your name.

3. Heavenly Father, I surrender myself to You afresh, please make me that man/woman, that You can use

to bring down the power and brilliance of Your of light amid darkness.

4. Heavenly Father, I surrender myself to You completely, please fill me with Your burden for my family, local church, and community.

5. Heavenly Father, I ask that by Your Holy Spirit, make me a man/woman of Your presence so I can experience Your salvation in my life and home over the powers of darkness.

6. Heavenly Father, I surrender myself to Your Holy Spirit, please teach me how to fight the good fight of faith and to pull down the strongholds of Satan against all that's good and godly in my life, family, business, local church, and community.

7. Heavenly Father, I willingly enlist myself to be a man/woman You can use in and for Your kingdom through the ministry of prayer in Jesus' name, AMEN!

Chapter Seven: The Whole Purpose of Prayer

Let us pray:

1. Heavenly Father, I ask that You ignite a passion within my soul, a craving to become like Jesus in words and deeds.

2. Heavenly Father, I ask that you fill me with Your Holy Spirit afresh and set me on my journey so I can become more and more like Jesus each day of my life.

3. Heavenly Father, I ask that You forgive me for relying on my own wisdom for direction. Today, I ask that You take the wheel and lead me into the place where I will fulfill Your destiny for my life.

4. Heavenly Father, You are the Only one, who knows where the pasture of life is greener and where the waters are still, please lead me on, and deliver me from making bad decisions and leading a wasteful life.

5. Heavenly Father, I ask that You sharpen my spiritual senses, so I can know how to exercise Your discernment as I navigate my journey here on earth. I want to know Your rest and enjoy the fruit of my labor.

6. Heavenly Father, please do not hide Your face away from me. Let Your face shine upon me, for it is by Your light that I see light, and show forth Your glory in the land of the living.

7. Heavenly Father, I ask that You deliver me from the shackles of prayerlessness, and pour upon me, the Spirit of Grace and Supplication so I can truly look upon You in Jesus' name, AMEN!

Chapter Eight: What Did Jesus Pray About?

Let us pray:

1. Heavenly Father, I come to You to ask for a fruitful understanding of the power of prayer.

2. Heavenly Father, today I come in repentance from my prayerlessness and pride in not calling upon Your name as I should nor seek to know and do Your will as I should.

3. Heavenly Father, today I submit myself to the pursuit of Your will and to do my best in doing Your will as far as I know according to Your power that works in me.

4. Heavenly Father, please fill me with Your Holy Spirit afresh today and help me to never go one more day without asking for the in-filling of the blessed Holy Spirit.

5. Heavenly Father, by the blood of Jesus Christ, I break every form of struggles and limitations over my life. Through Your Holy Spirit, please give me a daily experience of Your presence and power so my life can become the channel of Your blessings to everyone around me.

6. Heavenly Father, I submit my spirit, soul, and body to You. Please make my heart Your home; Please be everything I am and all I know; And search me through and through, until my life becomes the instrument You want it to be and the expression of the image of Christ in my family, local church, place of work, and community.

7. Heavenly Father, please make me a Son/Daughter in Your kingdom that calls upon Your name; Please help me to take my position amongst those who will bring the manifestations of Your power and glory in these

last days; Please deliver me from the grip of prayer-lessness and powerless Christian living until Your kingdom comes and Your will be done in my life in Jesus' name, AMEN!

The prayers listed above are not things you pray once and for all. No, those are prayers to make until you come into the experience of what you pray for, and you'll know when you do. Set a daily time aside to pray at least for an hour. Forget about your mundane needs and replace them with the ones above. Before too long, you'll see the strength of God flow into your heart; you'll notice that your prayer has changed. Your time of prayer will become something to look forward to, and the name of Jesus will become sweet again and effective in your mouth.

NOTES

1. E.M. Bounds, E.M. Bounds on Prayer (Peabody: Hendrickson Publishers Marketing, LLC, 2006), 172.

2. Richard Lea, "Spare Christopher Hitchens from Prayers," published September 2010 at The Guardian, https://www.theguardian.com/books/booksblog/2010/sep/20/christopher-hitchens-prayers.

3. Myles Munroe, The Fatherhood Principle (New Kensington: Whitaker House, 2008), 112.

4. E.M. Bounds, The Works of E.M. Bounds (Media: Reformed Church Publications, 2015), 112.

5. Martin Luther, A Mighty Fortress is Our God. "The United Methodist Hymnal." (Nashville: The United Methodist Publishing House, 1989), 110.

6. William Walford, Sweet Hour of Prayer. "The United Methodist Hymnal." (Nashville: The United Methodist Publishing House, 1989), 496.

7. Mike Lutz, "God Everyday: 365 Life Application Devotions (Online: Readhowyouwant.com Limited, 2014), 234.

8. Horatio G. Spafford, It Is Well with My Soul. "The United Methodist Hymnal." (Nashville: The United Methodist Publishing House, 1989), 377.

9. Jim Reeves, "Teach Me How to Pray," accessed August 26 at *https://www.lyrics.com/lyric/9340616/Jim+Reeves/Teach+Me+How+to+Pray*.

CPSIA information can be obtained
at www.ICGtesting.com
Printed in the USA
LVHW021921141122
732652LV00008B/359